PRENTICE-HALL
CONTEMPORARY PERSPECTIVES IN MUSIC EDUCATION SERIES
Charles Leonhard, Editor

PRENTICE-HALL INTERNATIONAL, INC., London
PRENTICE-HALL OF AUSTRALIA, PTY. LTD., Sydney
PRENTICE-HALL OF CANADA, LTD., Toronto
PRENTICE-HALL OF INDIA PRIVATE LTD., New Delhi
PRENTICE-HALL OF JAPAN, INC., Tokyo

the evaluation
of music teaching
and learning

RICHARD COLWELL
College of Education, University of Illinois

PRENTICE-HALL, INC., Englewood Cliffs, New Jersey

All rights reserved. No part of this book may be reproduced in any form or by any means without permission in writing from the publisher.

Printed in the United States of America

C-13-292151-0
P-13-292144-8

Library of Congress Catalog Card No.: 70-117013

Current Printing (last digit):

10   9   8   7   6   5   4   3   2

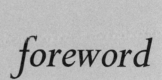

foreword

Contemporary Perspectives in Music Education is a new series of professional books for music education It establishes a pattern for music teacher education based on the areas of knowledge and processes involved in music education rather than on the levels and specializations in music education.

The areas of knowledge include philosophy of music education, psychology of music teaching, and research methods. The processes include program development, instruction, administration, supervision, and evaluation.

The basic premise of the series is that mastery of all of these processes and areas of knowledge is essential for the successful music educator regardless of his area of specialization and the level at which he teaches. The series presents in a systematic fashion information and concepts basic to a unified music education profession.

All of the books in the series have been designed and written for use in the undergraduate program of music teacher education. The pattern of the series is both systematic and flexible. It permits music education instructors at the college level to select one or more of the books as texts on the basis of their relevance to a particular course.

Early in his professional career Professor Colwell developed a consuming interest in the theory and technique of evaluation. This book is the result of a continuing quest on his part for insight and skill in the evaluation of music teaching and learning. The fact that he began this quest as a graduate student in music education at the University of Illinois is a source of great personal and professional satisfaction to me.

Evaluation has traditionally been an area of weakness in the music education program and in the preparation of music teachers. The current emphasis on achievement in the total educational program has made continuing neglect of evaluation in music education unthinkable.

Professor Colwell's contribution to Contemporary Perspectives in Music Education contains the information that music educators need to accomplish the task of evaluation rationally, systematically, objectively, and sympathetically. His extraordinary enthusiasm for music education and his understanding of the evaluative process are reflected in every page. In treating the evaluation of the total program of music education, he establishes a clear-cut distinction between evaluation and measurement and clarifies the relationship between the two processes. His comprehensive treatment includes curriculum evaluation as well as evaluation in the cognitive, psychomotor, and affective domains. The quality, comprehensiveness, and timeliness of this book establish it as a landmark in the continuing professionalization of music education.

Charles Leonhard

preface

This book is designed to set forth the principles of measurement and evaluation, and to relate these to the instructional processes in music. The purpose of the book is to show how evaluation, properly used, can improve any kind of teaching-learning situation. Evaluation is discussed not only in terms of tests but also in its broadest context, encompassing a host of devices as they pertain to music teaching at all levels from preschool through college. General principles as well as specific details of information are offered applicable to all forms of music instruction. The dominant concern is that evaluation is primarily a teaching tool, rather than a method for giving grades or an after-the-course appraisal.

A discussion of this subject as it applies to music is not possible without first determining what one expects to accomplish in music. The ultimate purpose of teaching music may well be an aesthetic outcome, or the grasping of a symbolic expression of the meaning of life, but music teaching must set up goals of knowledge and skill through which these aesthetic experiences can become a reality, then evaluate to discover how well the goals have been met. Thus, evaluation is related, first, to objectives and to the philosophy of the curriculum; second, to methodology and the organization of experiences and situations; and third, to the actual process of appraisal and its application. In order to cover all these important areas, the book treats evaluation in terms of three domains of educational objectives: cognitive, affective, and psychomotor.

The language of the book is nontechnical and concentrates on communicating an understanding of the uses and interpretation of evaluative tools. Emphasis is placed on the *what, how, when,* and *what for,* rather than on statistical intricacies of construction or application. The *what* refers to the devices or methods appropriate to particular musical objectives, in terms of both student and subject matter needs. The *how* describes techniques of evaluation, the unobtrusive as well as the scheduled measurement. Without the *how,* excellent devices lose all meaning. The *when* and *what for* continually reemphasize the role of evaluation in the improvement of the teaching-learning process. Though systematic evaluation has traditionally been neglected by music teachers, a thoughtful application of the information presented here can contribute to better music programs in the schools and, in time, to a more musically literate public.

An acknowledgement is due members of the tests and measurements classes of the University of Illinois for their criticisms of the manuscript, and to the author's wife, Ruth, whose perceptive editing of ideas as well as of the manuscript has made the writing of this book possible.

R.C.

contents

CHAPTER ONE

purposes of evaluation

INTRODUCTION

For the human being, the process of living requires the constant use of evaluation. Plants grow and thrive according to their nature, animals survive by instinct and training, but man adapts to and overcomes his environment by constantly saying to himself, "How am I doing?" then, "How can I do better?" The second question is essential for progress, but it is always preceded by the first question, and that is evaluation. We are occasionally successful when we act according to whim or instinct, but to be consistently successful, actions must stem from continual, intelligent evaluation in various life situations.

In freeway traffic, for example, the driver judges distance and speed, he evaluates the skill of the driver in the next lane, he estimates that driver's reaction time in stopping and starting. He may also estimate other factors in relation to driving: the other driver's ability to smoke, play the radio, tend the children, or show affection to his girl while coping with the hazards of the road.

Decision-making is often equated with evaluation. In one sense, the two are the same, for to evaluate is to make a decision concerning the quality of the thing being evaluated. Certainly, intelligent decisions cannot be made without the techniques of evaluation. In our present complicated society, the ability to make decisions is so valued that a new professional class has arisen whose job it is to understand and use the evaluative devices and to give advice based upon the findings. The ability to make complex and multiple decisions has become a standard for judging a person's worth to society; the man who can accurately size up the situation, evaluate pertinent factors, and make a sound decision is valued in business and industry, in government, in the military, and in education.

Evaluation is so pervasive, so much a part of our everyday lives, so necessary to intelligent human action, that its role is often overlooked. For example, there is at present a belief that American society would be improved by a greater understanding of the arts and that music is one essential area of the arts with which all educated persons should be familiar so that they can listen to and perform all types of music, understand it, and gain pleasure from it. However, this growing interest in the humanities and in general music has not yet included attention to some vital specifics. For example, what are the strengths of the present school music program? Where has the program failed? How much training in music would be necessary to give the average person that level of ability described above? What methods and materials are most useful in teaching general music successfully? These questions depend upon evaluation for their answers. Additional evaluation is needed to determine whether a general music and humanities emphasis in the public schools will indeed result in a fuller, richer life for those who come within its influence. Without a means for accurate judgment, the effectiveness of the arts can only be guessed. Since guesses are colored by personal bias, many valuable educational resources may be wasted and young persons deprived of the best educational opportunities while educators experiment on the basis of their own subjective opinions.

DEFINING EVALUATION

The use made of evaluation depends upon one's opinion as to what evaluation is and what its purposes are, one's expectations as to what it can do, and knowledge of the ways it can be effective in improving teaching and learning. It is often pointed out that evaluation can be a menace when it is used ignorantly or for the wrong purposes. However, in such cases the fault lies not with evaluation itself but with the inept handling of evaluative tools. Understanding the whys and wherefores of evaluation is necessary for successful teaching. Those who, through ignorance or because of bad experiences with evaluation, refuse to make use of it in their teaching are robbing themselves of a useful, even vital, tool.

What definition can be formulated for evaluation to show its applicability to the music education process? Evaluation is a judgment of the worth of an experience, idea, procedure, or product. The worth of anything can be judged in absolute terms, as when we say that music is good or great; such a judgment refers to the intrinsic quality of the thing in question. Worth can be in relationship to a purpose, as when we say that marches are good for parades; this judgment refers to the extrinsic value or usefulness of the thing in question without mention of its intrinsic worth. Thus, evaluation can be in either absolute or utilitarian terms, usually established prior to the act of evaluation and clear to the evaluator.

But evaluation in the schools is more than this. Evaluation is often defined as a judgmental process that systematically gathers information on a specified problem. Here the key word is *systematically*. Just as teaching needs to be in some pedagogical order for best results, and experiences need to be organized according to difficulty, interest, student readiness and so forth, so evaluation requires system and organization. Although evaluation can be spontaneous and informal, it is better when it is planned and purposeful. Even in this day of bulging classrooms and teacher shortages, no teacher would be rehired who selected reading materials because he liked the story, who introduced multiplication before number concepts were established, or who taught chord structure without any listening experience. Perhaps the schools will soon reach a stage of sophistication where teachers will also be penalized for giving a test because they are unprepared for the class period, for using a poor and hastily created examination, for pulling an inapplicable test out of the files, or for failing to use the results in a beneficial way.

To say that evaluation is a systematic process that collects data on a specified problem is still to leave the definition incomplete. The collection of data or information is not enough, for unless they are interpreted and disseminated, data can provide little evaluation. Data must be interpreted not only in terms of the specific problem, but also in terms of the discipline or subject matter area and the known research on the problem. The music teacher gives a test, either self-constructed or standardized, and dutifully records the scores in his gradebook. The music student attends a contest and receives a rating. If the test score and the rating remain only raw data without interpretation, the teacher and student may misunderstand what the score and rating mean. A bassoon player receives a I rating at a contest. All of the bassoonists at that particular contest receive I ratings. What meaning does this have? It may mean that this year all of the bassoonists were superior in quality; it may mean that the bassoonists were poor but showed marked improvement when compared with last year's bassoon performances; it may mean that the judge did not feel competent to evaluate bassoonists; or it might mean that bassoonists are scarce and so bassoon playing needs every possible encouragement. Without sufficient information, the I rating remains simply a rating and subject to a variety of erroneous interpretations. Similarly, classroom test scores need interpretation. A score of 95 can be considered an absolute standard for an A grade, evidence that the student has mastered the subject matter well. A 95 can be considered in relationship to the rest of this year's scores or to past scores. If other students score higher than 95, this requires a different interpretation from that of 95 as the highest grade. There are further fine points of differentiation. If 95 is the best grade, with other scores ranging from there down to 75, this leads to one conclusion; if 95 is the best grade, but the other scores range from 30 to 75, the 95 takes on another meaning.

The preceding illustrations point up the fact that the professional evaluator trained in educational psychology and measurement can only help with evaluation in a subject matter area; the specialist-teacher (in our case, the music teacher) must do the planning and interpret the results. The music teacher, therefore, needs a knowledge of evaluation techniques and methods, should have the ability to communicate with the measurement specialist and the computer programer, and must be able to understand and judge the systematic process of data treatment. Thus, a broad definition of educational evaluation is (1) the systematic process of collecting information, (2) the enlightened interpretation of the information, and (3) the dissemination of the results back into the teaching-learning situation. Each step of this process must be related to the specific problem for which evaluation is sought, the problem usually being stated in terms of behavioral objectives in order to provide an intelligent, responsible judgment about a process, an act, or an idea.

MEASUREMENT

Evaluation as a process is not synonymous with measurement. Measurement is one act, or one kind of act, in the total evaluation process. The small boy licking his ice cream cone on a hot summer afternoon evaluates his treat as satisfying, but he does not measure it unless another boy comes along with a larger one. Measurement is generally defined as the administering of a test or the making of a judgment in quantitative terms. The giving of an examination is measurement, as are tryouts for seat placement in the school orchestra. A complete evaluation program that includes no measurement is unlikely, but evaluation that consists solely of two or three tests given throughout a semester is inadequate. Standardized tests, such as those that test music aptitude or musical ability, are measures, but there are many other types of measurement. One can measure the number of notes in a phrase, the range of each instrument in the compositions of Ives, the number of fifth-grade children who recognize irregular meter in a Stravinsky composition, and so on. With some aid from psychologists, one can also measure attitude, opinion, and preference in music.

Because measurement has so often been equated with evaluation, music teachers have developed a number of misconceptions and fears concerning evaluation in general and have tended to avoid objective evaluation. One misconception is that music tests are unfair because they are culturally based and do not account for the differences in the cultural background of students. Tests differentiate among students who cannot read with equal ability, whose home environments provide varying kinds of musical stimuli, whose experiences give them unequal equipment in music. Music tests are culturally based in that music is learned and learning proceeds from the culture, but they are not for this reason unfair. Henry Dyer has said, "I wish we could get it out of people's heads that tests are unfair to the underprivileged and get it into their heads that it is the hard facts of social circumstance and inadequate education that are unfair to them."[1] Tests measure so that the teacher may have increased knowledge about the students. The opportunities for discrimination and unfairness arise in the teacher's use of the information rendered by the tests.

Other misconceptions suggested by Dyer include the idea that tests are infallible—or the opposite, that they are totally fallible. Test results are only an estimate or a prediction. To say that a test predicts is to say that it measures only a fraction of its subject, whether the subject be facts, skills, opinions, or beliefs; therefore, test results are a prediction of the individual's total grasp of facts, total array of skills, total set of opinions or beliefs for the matter under concern. Since tests only predict, their proper purpose is to help one make a decision. Even if a test is correct little more than half the time, one still makes better decisions

---

1 Henry Dyer, "Is Testing a Menace to Education?" *Readings in Educational and Psychological Measurement*, ed. Clinton Chase and H. Glenn Ludlow (Boston: Houghton Mifflin Company, 1966), p. 42. Reprinted from *New York State Education*, XLIX (October 1961).

with it than without it. The more efficient and accurate it is, the more useful it can be in arriving at sound decisions. The classroom music teacher asked to recommend fifth-grade students who may have potential for instrumental music will be surprisingly inaccurate in his judgments if these are based solely upon his observation of classroom participation. If he has in his gradebook a few scores from informal, teacher-constructed tests, his judgments will be more correct. If the school system gives standardized tests of musical aptitude and achievement, the process of predicting those students who will do well in instrumental music will be made more efficient and less subject to costly, disappointing mistakes.

Additional misconceptions about evaluation are: (1) that a single test can measure all music objectives, (2) that tests can only measure facts, (3) that only the nonmusical part of music can be measured by tests, and (4) that taking a test creates a negative impression in the students, which turns them against music. None of these is true, but most are sufficiently widespread that they have hindered the acceptance and use of tests as an integral part of public school music. Teachers fear that evaluation will have objectives other than their own, that students will be put in competition with each other, that the musical setting will be destroyed, that students will be motivated by grades rather than by the inherent values of music, that information will become an end in itself, that students will study the teacher and test rather than studying music. The basic fear behind these objections is that the teacher will be evaluated rather than the student. A major purpose of the present text is the dispelling of this traditional fear of evaluation in music; the belief has hindered rather than helped music education. The entire purpose of evaluation is to aid the learning process, not to find fault. The teacher who systematically evaluates his own teaching will not hesitate to welcome outside evaluation, for he is familiar with and understands the results.

THE GROWTH OF EVALUATION

In the lengthy history of music, evaluation has been both important and rigorous. Evaluation of musical performance dates back at least to the Olympic games of ancient Greece, where musicians, as well as athletes and poets, vied for the coveted laurel wreath, and the judgments were severe. Contests and folk festivals in which individuals and groups were judged upon their musical skill can be found in the age-old traditions of nearly every country. During the Middle Ages, admittance to the musical guilds was based on the display of some achievement or performance deemed meritorious by a panel of judges. Church and court musicians in the Renaissance and Baroque periods were subjected to rigorous tests when applying for positions of employment. All these instances pertain to the professional musician, but Elizabethan England offers overwhelming examples of the musical excellence of the cultured amateur—even monarchs were composers and performers—which leaves no doubt about the high standards imposed upon the child whose parents could afford music lessons. The gentleman or gentlewoman was expected to be able to take his or her part (often a rather demanding one by today's standards) in the musical recreation of the court or private home.

The impetus to modern educational testing was provided by men like Binet, Terman, and others who at the beginning of the twentieth century developed some of the first aptitude tests. Achievement testing was instituted in the schools in 1845, but the real start was not made until Thorndike's book on measurement appeared in 1904.[2] Even so, the use of such measures was limited until World Wars I and II created demands for massive training and education.

The tools initially developed for testing were guidance instruments such as intelligence tests and measures of performance ability in mechanical and physical skills. When standardized testing tools began to be utilized in the public schools, certain academic areas benefited more than others. A few music tests were standardized and published; school accrediting agencies established guidelines; and the Research Council of the Music Educators National Conference (MENC) published a seven-point checklist of evaluative criteria.[3] Some of these efforts were valuable; most were superficial and extraneous to the process of teaching. The exception was the music aptitude test, which found widespread use and was often helpful in the school music program.

EVALUATION'S CHANGING ROLE

Music evaluation in the university and conservatory has historically been well defined. The performing musician and the musical scholar have had to pass an extensive examination system: solo performance, written examinations over a variety of areas, ear-training tests of various kinds. The essentials in terms of both subject matter and skills have been carefully delineated; the musician has had no question as to what must

---

[2] Edward L. Thorndike, *An Introduction to the Theory of Mental and Social Measurements* (New York: The Science Press, 1904).

[3] "The Evaluation of Music Education," Marguerite Hood, chairman (Washington, D.C.: Music Educators National Conference, 1952).

be learned before he might be considered qualified to graduate from the university or conservatory. Dick's *Handbook of Examinations in Music,*[4] a British publication that went through nine editions from 1898 to 1912, is an example of the emphasis placed, around the turn of the century, upon passing tests in order to obtain the coveted diploma. During the first two decades of the twentieth century, a number of sight singing tests and theme recognition tests were developed, together with tests over factual information. These culminated in the *Kwalwasser-Ruch Test of Musical Accomplishment* and the *Beach Music Achievement Test* of the 1920s. Whether the examination during this period dictated the content of the music courses or reflected the current emphases of the courses cannot be determined, but it is evident that a close relationship existed between objectives, content, and evaluation.

After 1920, a change began to take place in the philosophy of school music. The uses, emphases, and content of school music shifted. The public school instrumental director appeared; the music educator became distinct from the musician, with a different course of training. With the exception of the band contest, interest in both objectives and evaluation decreased. The relationship among these events was more than coincidental. When music became an accepted part of the school day rather than an after-school function, its focus changed from interest in the talented few to an activity for all. By the 1940s, the new purposes for music in the school defined it as a recreation activity; hence, either music was not in need of measurement, or it was vocationally oriented for a select few, for whom evaluation meant primarily performance evaluation by the private teacher. Published tests existed in the 1920s and 1930s, but they were uneven in quality and often measured only facts. Music teachers failed to show interest in the creation of tests more appropriate to their purposes.

The various approaches to music teaching are reflected in the textbooks from different years. In texts from the 1930s, the emphasis was upon measurement, the use of tests, the tests available, and methods for creating quantitative devices to tabulate classroom experiences. As the pendulum swung away from emphasis upon drill, music reading, and performance, it swung toward *music as experiences,* the five-fold program of singing, moving, playing, creating, and listening. The new program offered no place for objective evaluation, because of the difficulty involved in measuring awareness, activity, enjoyment, and participation. A further reason for the exclusion of objective evaluation was the underlying belief that testing missed the point of musical learn-

---

[4] Ernest A. Dicks, *A Handbook of Examinations in Music* (London: Novello and Company Limited, 1898).

ing, that it did not get at the essentials, that it implied a rigorousness that detracted from the goals of spontaneity and pleasure in music. This viewpoint held sway for a decade; then in the 1950s, a few of the more thoughtful music educators began to suggest that the experience of music in the public schools was superficial and ineffective and produced disappointing results. Writers pointed to the importance of the aesthetic quality of the musical experience, stating that the focus of the experience should be the content of the music itself, not how music could contribute to good citizenship or leisure activities. As this emphasis became more widely accepted, it created a concern for evaluation that could measure understanding and appreciation—and those skills upon which understanding and appreciation depend. Evaluation again was included in the music education textbooks, if not in the music classroom.

Characteristic of the new approach, and perhaps the most effective and perceptive version of it, was the writing of Leonhard and House.[5] They argued that music deserved a place in the public schools only if it could be justified as offering something unique for the education of the individual.

Recently trained teachers in all fields have a knowledge of the numerous tools and techniques available for gathering information, and these teachers are showing the effectiveness of the new evaluative tools for learning. Hopefully, the music teacher will be a part of this enlightened concern; old prejudices will be abandoned and evaluation will assume the same central focus in music learning that it has in all intelligent actions.

The new and healthy interest in evaluation may be partially due to federal grants for educational research, which require evaluation of results; or interest may have arisen from the fact that more music teachers now enroll in graduate study than have in the past and find there an emphasis upon research and evaluation; the widespread attention to curriculum construction and revision may have stimulated awareness of evaluation's importance. Other reasons suggest themselves: Current research into how and when children learn illustrate the great need for evaluation at every step of the learning process. There is also an obvious growing concern over the unimpressive results that public school music has shown in the past, coupled with the desire to upgrade education in this area. Not the least important may be the realization that many organizations outside the school itself are becoming increasingly vocal about music's failings in the public school; the National Education As-

---

5 Charles Leonhard and Robert House, *Foundations and Principles of Music Education* (New York: McGraw-Hill Book Company, 1959).

sociation (NEA), the U.S. Office of Education, university-oriented symposiums (e.g., the Tanglewood and the Yale reports), curriculum directors, state arts councils, and others are concerned.

Attention to evaluation is related to new concerns, concerns of both students and teachers. The new concern on the part of the teacher is not so much for the welfare of the student—this has always been a characteristic of the good teacher—as it is for whether he is doing all he should to create the best learning situation. The teacher recognizes new areas of responsibility formerly felt to be beyond his domain: schedule, budget, facilities, methods of instruction, equipment, and the ways in which these interact with the learning process. These require evaluation. With evaluation, the student can help decide which areas of learning are important, where to invest his time as he looks ahead to college entrance or a vocation—this in contrast to the past when the student largely relied on others to tell him what to do and what course of study to follow.

THE RELATIONSHIP
BETWEEN OBJECTIVES AND EVALUATION

"The history of the standardized testing movement provides an excellent springboard for the more general study of educational goals, content and learning experiences, and organization of content. The process of evaluation appears to be very closely related to the establishment and evaluation of goals and objectives."[6] Unless goals are "clearly and firmly fixed in the minds of both parties (teacher and pupil), tests are at best misleading; at worst, they are irrelevant, unfair or useless."[7] Where objectives are not obvious, students will study the teacher and his idiosyncrasies, since these are easier to discern than the objectives and often just as reliable for obtaining a good grade. Many of the most important learnings from school are never purposely taught by the teacher; the crucial fact is that these important learnings may be negative as well as positive when the objectives are not well thought out or not clearly stated. Learning proceeds best when there is a close association between objectives and evaluation.

Objectives should clearly state *minimum* acceptable performance. In order to do this they must be stated in active terms. For example, one such objective might be the ability of each student to define and

---

[6] Clinton Chase and H. Glenn Ludlow, eds., *Readings in Educational and Psychological Measurement* (Boston: Houghton Mifflin Company, 1966), p. 1.

[7] Robert F. Mager, *Preparing Instructional Objectives* (Palo Alto, Calif.: Fearon Publishers, 1962), p. 4.

demonstrate *crescendo* and *ritard* at the end of the semester. Once the student has achieved an objective it becomes passive, with little power to influence the course of events. Thus, the objective provides a means of self-evaluation and self-satisfaction when it is sufficiently well defined to help the student see his own progress. Use must be made of short-range goals, on a daily or weekly or unit basis, to structure the learning experience for the student and provide a feeling of success to the learner and teacher. Goals of a broader, more encompassing nature provide guidance to the entire course or program and are the source from which intermediate objectives and appropriate learning activities are derived.

CRITERIA FOR OBJECTIVES

One of the most important uses of evaluation is to make value judgments about objectives. Most discussions of the relationship between evaluation and objectives refer to comparing actual achievement with the hoped-for achievement, or objective. But the objectives themselves must also be evaluated. To evaluate objectives implies not only the careful scrutiny of new ideas and trends but also the continued scrutiny of goals presently in use, in order to keep abreast of the changing world. "Time makes ancient good uncouth" is surely more true now than when Lowell wrote it

Evaluation presupposes a set of standards or criteria. What sort of standards can be found by which to judge the objectives set forth for the music program? The following list is one that the reader may wish to modify on the basis of his own experience and careful thinking, but it contains most of the criteria needed for evaluating the worth of any goal for music education. (1) The objective must set forth a musical achievement that can be learned. It should state what is to be taught and learned, not how it is to be taught and learned. (2) The objective must be stated in behavioral terms. (3) Within the statement of the objective one should be able to identify what constitutes minimum acceptable performance. If a goal is to be aimed for and attained, both student and teacher need to know at what point they can consider the goal as achieved. "Mastery of the instrument," then, is not a good objective; the first-year player thinks he has mastered the instrument, and the concert artist throws up his hands in frustration over some elusive trick of the instrument he longs to control. This statement needs to be translated into standards and conditions: the player can perform certain scales, arpeggios, embellishments, etc., at a certain speed; can produce a tone quality agreed upon as pleasant or adequate by two or more experts; can sight-read pieces at a certain specified level of difficulty; and so forth. (4) The objective should offer the potentiality for measuring or evaluating its achievement. Such terms as *awareness, appreciation,* and *understanding* cannot be objectively taught for, measured, or evaluated unless redefined in more precise language. Even if the awareness is specified or the understanding is specific, there may be no agreement on what awareness or understanding means, since these terms can imply a simple concept or an extremely complex ability, depending upon the frame of reference used. (5) The objective must be one that is considered important by those involved with the planning and that will contribute to a higher level of objectives or lead to continuing growth. (6) The objective should be sufficiently unique that it is not covered by or contained in some other objective. When the second and third criteria are observed, it is easier to determine what area of achievement is included in an objective and what is excluded. Only when objectives remain unclear do they overlap, contradict each other, or leave gaps in the learning that are unaccounted for. (7) The objective must be of the proper level of difficulty. Is there reasonable hope of accomplishing it? If the students have not achieved at this level, has such achievement taken place in a sufficiently large number of public schools to indicate its feasibility? Is the objective so easy that it offers little challenge to the students? Does it include more than what has been done and what is known already? The proper level of difficulty is probably the area where teachers are most timid. They are skeptical about the potential achievement of the students in their classes, and they dwell on the limitations of time, equipment, previous backgrounds, and insufficient staff that hinder the achievement of really challenging goals. If the goal is set a little out of reach and real effort made to attain it, this practice will in a few years radically upgrade the music program and the musical learning of the students. (8) Finally, the objective must be in terms of the individual child and his needs. The materials to be used and the experiences to be undergone are not to be selected in light of the teacher's preference solely, though this undoubtedly enters in. There are better performances and poorer performances, better music and poorer music; standards are important today, but they must not obliterate such educational principles of learning as order, interest, recognition, and fulfillment.

USES FOR EVALUATION

Education is big business, and expensive business. When an item is expensive, there is usually a demand for proof of its value and justification of the expense. The teenager yearning for an electric guitar or a motorbike will have to do more planning and persuading than if he asked for a ukulele or a tennis racket. One justification for education is that it is important business for the nation—both government and industry need skilled, creative persons in increasing numbers. As the school has become more important and more expensive, increased demands and expectations have been placed upon it by society. With the pressures to show evidence of teaching and learning, evaluation becomes the source of authority and the frame of reference by which to compare the good with the less good.

Skepticism concerning evaluation is difficult to explain in the musician, since the performer is evaluated regularly—at his lessons and in recitals and concerts. The composer is judged at the first performance of his composition and at every succeeding performance of it. The teacher has customarily accepted the fact that he is judged on the performances of his groups, but recently the tendency has been to minimize such occasions. He finds music contests unprofitable and substitutes instead the music festival with its absence of competition; there is a trend towards excusing poor performance in concerts with the justification that it is educationally unsound to spend the time required to make the works flawless. He maintains that the rehearsal situation shows the public a more honest face. Concerts are programed for the undiscriminating rather than for the connoisseur. The teacher thus minimizes his performance objectives, but at the same time he often fails to set up evaluative processes for those other objectives (understanding, knowledge, appreciation, or whatever) that he has substituted for performance skill. As a result, he falls short of the effective teaching he could achieve with honest, concerned evaluation.

It is true that there are some outcomes of a good music program that are presently impossible to evaluate, but this fact does not excuse the music teacher from scrutinizing those areas that do lend themselves to evaluation. The argument is that previously stated: though the tools are limited, better decisions are made when the tools are used than when they are not. If only half of the objectives of the music program lend themselves to a sound evaluation program, better teaching is possible because the evaluation is done and the information used. The idea is frequently put forth that the real benefits of musical instruction will not appear for several years and that concurrent evaluation misses the point altogether. A similar statement is that real understanding of music comes only with intensive study and listening and that the public school music teacher's responsibility is only to introduce the student to music, to help him discover whether he wishes to pursue it intensively outside the school situation. These latter two ideas must be labeled as excuses for poor teaching; they do not and cannot reflect the objectives of a sound music program. They cannot be taken seriously as reasons for avoiding systematic evaluation.

EVALUATION IN THE INDIVIDUAL LEARNING PROCESS

Traditionally, the best way to teach music has been through the private music lesson. Leopold Mozart gently but firmly led his small son through the intricacies of composition and performance. Liszt attentively heeded Czerny's instructions. Even for these prodigies the indispensable foundations were laid through private tutoring from great teachers. Not only performers and composers but also consumers have learned to understand music, if not to create or re-create it, through the private lesson. Even public school music teachers, whose vocational aims minimize performance, are taught largely through private instruction. No other teaching approach has yet supplanted the private lesson. There is some justification for the assumption that the private lesson is an effective way to teach music. Ideally the half-hour of teacher-student interaction is filled with evaluation. The student performs and is criticized, praised, and guided in terms of objectives that both he and the teacher understand. What is expected and what is acceptable are clarified verbally or by demonstration. Further assignment of studies or music to perform and the way in which these are to be approached are specified on the basis of what the student can do now and what will help him progress. No prearranged set of tasks is given to him to be completed upon a prearranged time schedule; the entire crux of individual instruction is individual guidance based upon individual evaluation. The private teacher may believe himself to be just as opposed to testing as the public school music teacher, but he is constantly evaluating as he teaches, and he can do so successfully without tests or measures because he focuses his attention upon one student at a time.

The classroom teacher is not so fortunate. Class instruction greatly complicates the teacher's task of promoting individual learning. The changes that have come about in the teaching of music have largely been in the direction of group instruction in performance areas: class piano, class voice, class violin, and class wind instruments. Also, a widespread attempt to teach musical understanding without performance or with only a modicum has appeal, as general music classes demonstrate. These changes warrant a commensurate change in the musician's attitude toward evaluation in the learning process. Class instruction may have little value for the individual student; it may leave behind the slow student, it may condemn the talented to boredom and apathy, and it may confuse the average student through failure to clarify those points on which he has questions. This is particularly true in the music class where the student often does not know what the goals are or what achievement is expected of him.

Evaluation is of real importance to the student and to his endeavors to achieve. We have often heard the saying that ignorance is not serious, but that ignorance concerning one's own ignorance is fatal. If the student does not know that he does not know, he surely cannot even start on the road to learning. The very young child will say "I can swim!" or "I can play the piano!" because he is in the pool or at the keyboard. The older child may "take music" in school and presume he is learning music because he is in the music classroom, with never a glimmer of light into the abyss of his own ignorance. Failure in the teaching-learning situation occurs in programs in which objectives are so vague that they cannot be evaluated systematically, for the most effective way to know whether or not you know is through a valid evaluation process carefully based upon the objectives. In music programs that still advocate the objectives of awareness, positive attitude, musical understanding, enjoyment of good music, or other equally nebulous goals, evaluation is difficult, and it is almost impossible for the student to know whether he knows.

The public school student has regular music classes from grade 1 through grade 6 or 7, and for a healthy percentage of students, sufficient interest is created during those classes that they elect further music in grades 8 through 12. The student takes music in good faith, as he takes typing or biology, believing that he is learning what he needs to know. Later in life, he discovers the real quality of his musical education, whether he can carry his part independently in the civic chorus, whether he can teach himself to play the guitar, whether his chamber music colleagues have to correct his rhythm, whether an unfamiliar symphony can be comprehended with enjoyment, whether he can harmonize at the piano for his children or his friends.

The amateur who discovers inadequacy in his musical background can accept it casually; the student who goes to college planning a musical career and finds that he has numerous areas of ignorance has cause for concern. Most colleges and universities find freshman students woefully lacking in ear training and theory skills, and in an understanding of musical style. In short, these students do not know how to listen to music or how music is constructed—and what is music to him who cannot hear it with comprehension and intelligence? Lacking these skills, what has led the aspiring young person to hope for a musical career? Most likely he has become a good performer because he took private lessons where he was subject to continuous sympathetic evaluation. His performance skills are high, his musical skills low, because the general music program failed to evaluate his progress. Though his music teachers in the schools may have been good at planning lessons, explaining ideas, or making the classes interesting, their lack of knowledge about the student's progress hindered their successful teaching.

For the individual learning process, evaluation may be used to teach, not just to appraise. Tests have real potential for aiding learning because of the value placed upon them by the student; though he may feel resentful or indignant over tests, he *is* moved to action by them. Examinations often structure the course more definitely and show the relevance of the various parts of the course better than does the teacher's outline. If test questions are primarily on the dates of composers' lives and the names of their compositions, these will receive the attention, regardless of how much the teacher stresses in class the design of the phrase, the use of effective devices, or the pattern of harmonic rhythm. Teachers often seem to feel that if they prepare brilliant lectures, select vivid illustrations, and emphasize important points, they can afford to be haphazard about evaluation because the students will have learned the vital ideas in class. Unfortunately, nothing could be further from the truth. The teaching sequence is comparable to a boat with a leak: no matter how strong the craft, the spot upon which survival depends gets the attention.

Over a decade ago, Thorpe stated a case for evaluation in music.[8] He said that progress toward a goal can be meaningful only when the student understands the goal and his progress toward that goal. In music, as in other subjects, learning proceeds most efficiently when the student becomes competent enough to discern his own errors and deficiencies. In the classroom it is nearly impossible for the teacher to correct all the errors, and this is especially true where the learning situation is performance-oriented, as a band, orchestra, or chorus. No one's ear is acute enough to hear all the errors, and if it were, there would be no sensible way in which one could help each individual student correct his mistake and understand why it occurred. The problem is increased by the various levels of music experience and skill represented by any performing group. Some students are trying to read the notes or remember the fingering while others are concerned with tone quality or expressive devices. None of these things may be what the teacher wishes to focus upon at the particular moment.

With the current emphasis on teaching music through performance, use of standardized tests is almost mandatory. They are the most prac-

8 Louis Thorpe, "Learning Theory and Music Teaching," *Basic Concepts in Music Education,* Fifty-seventh Yearbook of the National Society for the Study of Education, ed. Nelson B. Henry (Chicago: University of Chicago Press, 1958), Chapter 7.

tical, efficient, and useful means of determining what each student knows. In large performing groups where the age span may be as much as four years, the teacher requires norms by age, grade level, and type of instrument to determine the progress of individuals. Such norms are usually available only on standardized tests.

Devices that recognize the difficulties of group teaching and incorporate immediate feedback have a place in the music program. Musicians have long recognized the pain of practicing incorrectly and then having to rectify their learned mistakes. Programed learning capitalizes on the immediate recognition of error and continual evaluation of performance, where the individual acts, then checks his action by comparing his performance with the correct one.

Finally, evaluation is important in motivation. When a young student feels he has learned a new thing or made progress toward a goal of value, he'll go home and tell his family what he has learned in music class. Later he will become more sophisticated, but the process will continue to have validity. Motivation that comes from within is possible when an attainable goal is recognized, when the method for attaining it is at least partially understood, and when knowledge is available along the way of one's progress toward the goal.

CURRICULUM EVALUATION

Evaluation is essential in the area of program building. In recent years the educational scene has been crowded with innovation: new ways to teach, new devices and machines to aid teaching, new areas of subject matter valuable to the expanding mind, and new insights to be found in traditional subject matter. Decisions must be made as to the pertinence of any or all of these innovations. How about the Kodály method? Do we want the Orff instruments? Can the Suzuki approach work for us? Is having general music in the high school better than having a junior chorus? Will students really get more out of a humanities course than out of a traditional music appreciation course? Will some of the bright students in the band actually learn theory from a certain set of programed tapes and workbooks? Should we not enter contests next year and have a city-wide music festival instead? New methods, like new discoveries, must be carefully evaluated to determine their advantages and disadvantages. If a new curriculum is as good as, or only slightly better than, the existing one, there is little cause for change. The profession must concern itself with finding out the kind, amount, and quality of change a program innovation will effect in learning. A host of questions can be assembled that should be asked concerning any educational innovation and that should be answered not by the spontaneous judgment of the innovator or by the subjective reactions of a few concerned individuals, but by data supplied from a varied evaluative program.

In program planning and building, checks are necessary at each step of instruction to ascertain progress toward the goal, to determine not only emphasis and relevancy but timing. Using evaluation in curriculum building is like using a map for traveling the highways; in unfamiliar territory one checks frequently to see where he is, to see if he is still on the road to the objective, to estimate whether he will arrive on time. Before starting the trip the traveler decides upon a reasonable route to the destination and totals the approximate mileage and the time it will take. Having done this, he uses the map as he goes along to revise or corroborate his original decisions as to route and time. The less routine the trip, the more at stake, the more carefully will he plan in advance and check his map as he proceeds. Likewise in learning, the more important the objective the more often checks should be made on appropriateness of method, progress toward goals, and arrival at intermediate objectives.

The term *curriculum evaluation,* as it is currently being used, refers to evaluating the methods of instruction and the effects of the process of instruction, rather than to concentrating solely upon end results. Curriculum is defined as the ongoing teaching-learning process rather than, as traditionally, a course of study. Curriculum evaluation is concerned with patterns or models by which the learning situation can be observed, described, discussed, and measured. These models furnish categories in which the various parts of the learning situation can be placed to clarify the process and make it easier to talk about, such categories as antecedents, transactions, outcomes.[9] The evaluation that uses these patterns or models is largely informal and descriptive; it can provide a penetrating and insightful measurement of the process of education, but it should always be accompanied by as much objective data as can be assembled. Curriculum evaluation is misleading to many; it appears to be a means for successfully avoiding objective measurement, or at least relegating it to a minor role, while accomplishing a careful evaluation couched in descriptive terms. One should accept with caution the claim made for curriculum evaluation that it is broadening the horizons of evaluation. In reality it is little more than astute and comprehensive interpretation of data gathered through observation. The evidence is still gathered in a systematic way based upon objectives and upon behaviors as these relate

---

[9] Robert E. Stake, "The Countenance of Educational Evaluation," *Teachers College Record,* LXVIII, 7 (April 1967).

to the objectives. This description of evaluation as a combination of observation and testing based upon goals and performed in a careful, systematic fashion is the original and traditional meaning for evaluation. Rather than broadening the horizons, curriculum evaluators have helped educators return to the original meaning of the process that has been narrowed by some to focus upon tests, test scores, and testing situations. Curriculum evaluators serve to remind us that evaluation must be in terms of the total learning situation beginning with formulation of the goals and continuing through the termination of the evaluative process itself.

One model will serve to illustrate how curriculum evaluation proceeds. The *CIPP* model (context, input, process, product), designed by Stufflebeam,[10] is a four-step process: (1) *context evaluation,* used when a project is first planned; (2) *input evaluation,* used immediately after context but during the planning phase; (3) *process evaluation,* used during the time the project is being conducted; and (4) *product evaluation,* usually applied after the conclusion of the project. In step 1, the evaluator identifies and defines the type of person to be taught, the needs of the population, the resources available, the teacher attitudes, and similar items. The second step is not actually separate, as Stufflebeam outlines it, but rather is an interpretation of the first step. The evaluator determines how best to use resources; he identifies possible strategies and research designs; he anticipates problems. In music curriculum evaluation, this continual need to relate the conditions of learning to evaluation requires a fund of information about how children learn music, how children become musical, and what conditions facilitate musical learning. Step 3, process evaluation, provides the continual flow of information back to the investigator. He is alert for the items he expects, but also attempts to collect unanticipated results. Step 4, product evaluation, is the step in which the evaluator defines objectives in operational terms, measures criteria in terms of the objectives, compares the outcomes with predetermined standards and analyzes project results in terms of the context, input, and process information. Decisions and judgments are made on the basis of product evaluation as it is partially based on information from the first three steps.

Evaluation can thus provide a framework in much the same way that objectives do in structuring curriculum. Because evaluation and objectives cannot be severed, their functions cannot be separated. Where objectives are established for different levels, there must also be cor-

---

[10] Daniel Stufflebeam, "Evaluation as Enlightenment for Decision Making," *Improving Educational Assessment of Measures of Affective Behavior,* ed. Wolcott H. Beatty (Washington, D.C.: NEA, 1969).

responding levels of evaluation. Evaluation schemes and devices useful for one level of objectives may be inappropriate for another.

Although new schools and even new school systems come into existence with some frequency, it is still true that only a small proportion of teachers and administrators can build their curriculum from scratch, setting up objectives and goals, then proceeding in logical fashion to create the program that will attain those ends. For most, curriculum construction is really reconstruction, with the inevitable struggle against tradition, inertia, habit, and preconceived opinion. The only way to know whether the new is genuinely superior to the old is to evaluate and to use the results in an objective fashion for making further alterations in the curriculum.

EVALUATION IN RESEARCH

Evaluation is an integral part of research as well as of teaching. The casual observer may be able to see more readily the uses of evaluation in research than in teaching; to the critical observer of the music field, both areas appear haphazard and unfocused when not aided by the discipline of evaluation.

To conceive of a good research study that does not require evaluation is almost impossible, and many good research designs are almost totally devoted to evaluating some aspect or phase of music teaching or learning. Where the researcher is not equipped to understand evaluation techniques, the value of the research is curtailed, since judgments are either omitted or made subjectively. Whether a study deals with the reasons for dropouts from instrumental music, a comparison of the effects of the Kodály and Orff systems, or the collection of French music appropriate for teaching elementary class music, evaluation and judgments have to be made. Similarly, research in philosophical and musicological areas demands the same sort of systematic, analytical evaluation, even though measurement may not be appropriate. If a school system wishes to determine the value of a contemporary music project, a composer-in-residence program, or an all-city festival, appropriate tools can and should be found for a systematic gathering of data and for careful interpretation of the results. Subjective evaluation, the filling in of checklists, using unexamined opinion, a relaxed and a careless attitude on the part of teacher or administrator militate against the discipline necessary in any worthwhile effort.

College curricula for the preparation of music teachers, together with textbooks in music education, have by omission contributed to the neglect of evaluation. Test and measurement courses, where taught, are often a general requirement for all prospective teachers and contain no specific focus upon music. The instances where no such course is taught leave the teacher trainee without even a general knowledge of evaluation, for the methods courses in music—elementary, secondary, general, instrumental, vocal—seldom give evaluation more than a passing nod. Similarly, the textbooks in the field fulfill their obligation by devoting a chapter or so to mode, median and mean, musical aptitude, and the shortcomings of the true-false test. Failure to show evaluation as an integrated, ongoing part of the teaching-learning process has resulted in inferior research as well as in a complacency born of ignorance, a belief that activities and experiences bring the desired results, and the avoidance of careful scrutiny that would determine whether or not the desired results were indeed occurring. Evaluation has become something nice to do, for those persons who are interested in that sort of thing and have a generous allotment of time in which to include such activities.

THE PROCESS OF EVALUATION

The process of evaluation has been described in a variety of ways, differing mainly in the terminology used. One description that seems to come close to the heart of the matter is shown in the following diagram. The diagram is in the form of a wheel, indicating that evaluation should be a circular process, each stage contributing to the next one and essential to it. The process centers around musical problems, for these are the content of the curriculum, and the last step of the evaluation process contributes to the succeeding first step, for planning the next musical experiences should be guided by the information derived from preceding evaluation. For the sake of clarity, it must be pointed out that "planning the next musical experiences" implies the use of objectives; the objectives must be referred to, interpreted in behavioral terms, and utilized in the selection of further learning experiences based upon evaluation. Conversely, the collection and interpretation of the data must be in reference to the same objectives used for planning the experiences.

The circular process of planning and teaching musical experiences, collecting the data, processing and interpreting the data, and disseminating and using the information applies specifically to the teacher-evaluator. The process is slightly different if the evaluator is someone from outside the classroom—supervisor, consultant, or administrator. In this instance, the first step of planning and presenting learning experiences is replaced by planning the evaluative tools and procedures; interpretation of data may require the help of the teacher and others. The responsi-

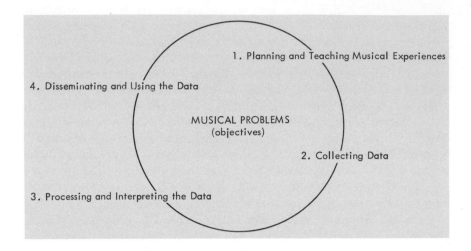

1. Planning and Teaching Musical Experiences

4. Disseminating and Using the Data

MUSICAL PROBLEMS
(objectives)

2. Collecting Data

3. Processing and Interpreting the Data

bility of using the information will again fall to the teacher; therefore his information must be complete and his understanding of it adequate.

Because objectives and evaluation are so closely related, there is a temptation to carry the circular diagram of the evaluative process too far and assume that evaluation is used in the selection of objectives. This is true only in the sense that evaluation must be used to determine which objectives to stress, to discover which objectives have been neglected and need additional emphasis, to learn how much progress still needs to be made towards any given objective. The objectives themselves should not be selected on the basis of information gathered through evaluation. Objectives are based upon, and draw their strength from, a philosophy of music education, a theory of what elements are important for well-balanced music education at any given level of growth. Objectives are not valid when based upon tradition, the practice of what is easy or entertaining, or what seems to fit the community or the overall school program. The selecting or establishing of objectives rests first with the thinkers and philosophers; the discipline of music, like all other disciplines, has certain standard content, which is recognized universally and is universally taught. In this sense, then, the music teacher does not determine objectives. He recognizes the universally accepted objectives of the discipline and attempts to work towards each of them, in terms appropriate for his own situation, making use of evaluative tools to discover where his students are in relation to the objectives and what degree of progress they make towards the goals. On the other hand, valid or successful programs of music education may vary somewhat from each other because of differences in equipment, in teacher strengths and weaknesses, in community culture, in time allotment, and similar factors. The sensible teacher will analyze his own abilities and capitalize on what he can do best while he is attempting to overcome weaknesses in his own musical equipment. He will consider the amount of time he has to work with a group of students, and the tools available for learning, as he plans goals and selects learning experiences. Basically, he must adhere to the objectives required for the discipline of music, but the emphasis given these may vary according to those factors mentioned above. In addition, the teaching approaches used to promote progress in learning will vary even where the goals remain the same. Generally, the development of performance skills, of good attitudes, and of interest receives more attention in the early years of school music than at the higher levels, where knowledge and understanding are emphasized. Learning experiences must be planned so that progress toward the objectives can occur as easily and painlessly as possible, building upon the present strengths and tendencies of the students, but continually keeping in mind the entire gamut of objectives.

QUESTIONS FOR DISCUSSION

1. What seem to be the primary reasons evaluation is not used in classrooms and performing groups?
2. What effect on music instruction is the national assessment program or newer testing devices having?
3. What evidence is required to convince musicians that additional evaluation will improve instruction?
4. Discuss the evaluation aspects of a curriculum, title I, or title III study.
5. What evaluation criteria should be used initially in determining objectives?
6. Is evaluation also appropriate for long range goals, and if so, who should assume the responsibility?
7. In what ways may evaluation be effective without objectives, and in what ways may objectives serve a purpose without evaluation?
8. What important *musical* objectives seem to be most compatible with the normal concept of evaluation?
9. Describe the trend in evaluation of music in a school system with which you are familiar.

REFERENCES

Ahmann, J. Stanley, and Marvin Glock, *Evaluating Pupil Growth* (2nd ed.). Boston: Allyn and Bacon, Inc., 1963, Chapter 1.

Berg, Harry, ed., *Evaluation in Social Studies,* Thirty-fifth Yearbook of the National Council for the Social Studies. Washington, D.C.: National Council for the Social Studies, 1965, Chapters 1–2.

Chase, Clinton, and H. Glenn Ludlow, eds., *Readings in Educational and Psychological Measurement.* Boston: Houghton Mifflin Company, 1966, Chapters 3, 5.

Dressel, Paul, et al., *Evaluation in Higher Education.* Boston: Houghton Mifflin Company, 1961, Chapters 2–3.

Grobman, Hulda, *Evaluation Activities of Curriculum Projects.* Chicago: Rand McNally & Co., 1968.

Gronlund, Norman, *Measurement and Evaluation in Teaching.* New York: The Macmillan Company, 1965, Chapter 3.

Henry, Nelson, ed., *Basic Concepts in Music Education,* Fifty-seventh Yearbook of the National Society for the Study of Education, Part I. Chicago: The University of Chicago Press, 1958, Chapter 13.

Mager, Robert, *Developing Attitude Toward Learning.* Palo Alto, Calif.: Fearon Publishers, 1968.

———, *Preparing Instructional Objectives.* Palo Alto, Calif.: Fearon Publishers, 1962.

Popham, W. James, et al., *Instructional Objectives.* Chicago: Rand McNally & Co., 1969.

Stodola, Quentin, and Kalmer Stordahl, *Basic Educational Tests and Measurement.* Chicago: Science Research Associates, Inc., 1967, Chapter 3.

Tyler, Ralph, Robert Gagné, and Michael Scriven, *Perpectives of Curriculum Evaluation.* Chicago: Rand McNally & Co., 1967.

CHAPTER TWO

selecting and administering evaluative tools

EVALUATION IN THE CLASSROOM

Much current discussion is concerned with evaluation programs in music education, but a *program* of evaluation is exactly what the profession has not had. A program implies that there is order, system, planning, and follow-up. Where there is an evaluation program one can expect to find cumulative records that provide a history of the student's progress in various areas and his most recent level of achievement. Each teacher would not have to begin in ignorance of the situation and the students, but would have written records to guide his planning and instruction. For many music educators, evaluation is synonymous with testing, and the purpose of testing has been confined to giving grades. This connection between testing and grades is especially unfortunate, for the relationship is far from direct. Where grades are of little importance, evaluation does not become unimportant. Evaluation is unimportant only where learning is also unimportant.

Often, grades have been the sole source of feedback to the student and his parents. In the process of giving grades, the teacher has been forced to consider the student's strengths and weaknesses, but because this is done only at the end of the year's program it is a post mortem act; it provides no feedback that can be used in the ongoing program of teaching and learning. When the next year's classes start, the teacher has no use for his old evaluations in the new situation but starts afresh with activities designed to interest the youngsters and fill the time. A major value of testing and measuring is in the feedback. Both teacher and student can continually assess progress. In programed learning or computer-assisted instruction, testing is continual, but there is no question of grade, simply of learning. Within such programs, however, there is still room for periodic testing covering large units of learning. These tests allow for assimilation, for establishing meaningful relationships between facts and ideas, and for problem-solving in depth. So grades can be minimized or abolished, but evaluation remains critical in learning.

In at least two areas, musicians are alert to evaluation and measurement. The performing musician continually attends to his own technique and musicianship, painstakingly polishing each phrase; he is cognizant of every flaw in attack, tone, intonation, or precision. The musicologist is equally aware of measurement. His standards of scholarship are exacting, and he brooks few exceptions. Certain skills of language and research are expected, for which the student in musicology makes rigorous preparation. A high level of knowledge is required, and it is tested for over and over from the undergraduate level through the doctor's degree. Why are music educators careless and seemingly unconcerned about the achievement of goals? Perhaps because they so often deal with children rather than with people old enough to have mastered musical skills and knowledges that can be challenged. In other public school areas, however, teachers are concerned with real progress rather than with pleasant experiences.

CRITERIA FOR SELECTING APPROPRIATE TESTS

Once it is decided that testing is to be a part of the music program, care must be exercised in selecting appropriate tools. All tests have value when properly used, but some tests are better than others, and some will be more suitable for certain stages or situations. Only a small part of music can be taught in any one year's program, no matter how superficial the treatment. Both common sense and experience verify this. Decisions as to the subject matter and objectives for the year's program imply decisions of measurement. Once these decisions have been made, the succeeding steps follow logically. In selecting published tests or in creating new ones, the features to consider are usability, reliability, and validity. Other data-gathering instruments, such as questionnaires and checklists, also need to be selected or constructed with these same features in mind.

USABILITY

Usability is the common sense consideration of ease in administering and scoring an evaluation device. Factors to be considered include: the equipment needed to administer the test (tape recorder, record player, opaque projector, piano); the time needed to administer it, including giving instructions and passing out necessary forms and special marking pencils; whether the test can be given by section if necessary; how difficult or time-consuming the scoring; the cost of the test to purchase and to score by machine. Each of these should be considered in the selection of an appropriate device. Anything worth doing in the classroom is going to take time, effort, and resources, both monetary and physical. Any evaluation will displace some other activity that is also beneficial, since it is patently impossible to do all of the worthwhile things. The question then is whether a specific testing effort is the right one. Testing does take time and money, and this must be realized at the outset. Further, the best use is made of a test when it can be planned for well in advance, so that its full value as a motivating factor and a teaching device can be utilized.

TIME

The decision to use standardized tests in the music program may find the teacher initially unprepared to make a choice of tests or to know how much time should be allotted for a systematic testing program. A workable approach to the problem is to plan the year's program, or even a two- or four-year program, decide what published tests are relevant to the goals and will augment the other evaluation devices, then allocate a certain percentage of time for the evaluative process. Students learn much from taking a test. Preparing for it, the actual test itself, and the review that follows as test answers are discussed and explained are an effective part of learning. Therefore, 10 to 25 percent of class time can be given to evaluation without jeopardizing educational goals but rather facilitating learning. With a definite allotment of time for evaluation, the usability of a test can be estimated with respect to other planned measures.

Not only the total time a test requires, but also the amount of time needed on a single day must be considered. Can the test be given in the regular music period? If not, can it be easily divided to fit into two or more periods? Will taking the test in several parts cause problems that will affect the validity of the test? Such factors as the possibility of students looking ahead and preparing for later questions, students marking on the test booklets that are given to other students for the next test session, and the time consumed in passing test blanks back by name affect the testing situation. If a test was standardized with students taking the entire test at once, the norms may be inaccurate for a situation in which the test is taken in two, three, or four parts. An alteration in the school day's schedule to allow for testing may create problems with other teachers who feel they cannot afford to give up the time. A major alteration of schedule in order to give a test is rarely justified.

ADMINISTRATION

A second aspect of usability is how difficult the test is to administer. Securing a tape recorder or a record player for a test should be no problem in the contemporary school. Problem equipment would be specialized devices such as audiometers for hearing tests, oscilloscopes for some types of tone measurement, tachistoscopes for music reading, and similar devices. However, equipment is not the only element presenting administrative problems. Individual tests are of great value but are difficult to administer. If the music period is a rehearsal for eighty-five orchestra members, a situation where eighty-four of them tootle, scrape, and pound while one is being tested has little merit. There are ways of getting around this, of course—a responsible person can administer the test in another room while the teacher conducts the regular rehearsal minus the one member being evaluated. Even so, a fifteen-minute individual test is very time-consuming. If a group measure can be found that correlates well with the skill being tested, the teacher is wise to select the group tool. Music is a subject that is never covered completely. The teacher must give ample time to evaluation, but he should not squander time on one method of testing if a shorter one may be substituted successfully.

Seating arrangements or writing surfaces required for a test may make the test difficult to administer. Long, involved directions may also make it difficult to administer. The need for the examiner to have some piano skill is part of at least one published test, and where the teacher lacks this he must find a competent, willing pianist or forego the test.

COST

The cost of the test may, but should not, be a major factor in its selection. Consideration should be in terms of value received. The largest outlay of money is the initial one for tapes or records, manuals, scoring templates, and test booklets or answer sheets. Answer sheets are relatively cheap, extremely cheap in terms of the benefits derived from them. If a good, appropriate test is purchased, it can be used for several years and possibly in several different kinds of music classes, so that the only continual cost lies in answer sheets and perhaps machine scoring. Administrators are accustomed to paying as much as one dollar per student to score some of the extensive batteries that have become standard. If the administrator is convinced that the music testing program is a sound one, beneficial to a large number of students, he will seldom object to the expense.

SCORING

The scoring system must be considered as a factor in the test's usability. Most tests can now be scored by machine. Machine scoring can provide a wealth of information in addition to the score, such as comparisons of part scores for individuals and groups, or comparisons of scores with selected attributes of the group or individual. Hand scoring systems require the use of a template, and some types of template are more efficient than others, though all hand scoring is time-consuming and fatiguing for the busy teacher. One type of template to avoid, if possible, is that which lines up next to the answers for comparison of letter or numbers; this is much slower and less accurate than the template that fits over the answer sheet.

TEST FORMS

Where more than one form of the test is available, this can be a factor in usability. Some tests are published in a regular form and in a short form. One music aptitude test presently available has a version that takes one hour and a second version that takes ten minutes. The short form might be more usable, but it invariably suffers in reliability.

BALANCE

An additional factor in usability is the need to maintain balance between various kinds of tests and evaluative tools. An aptitude test given once to each child may be important in guidance and placement. From the various published achievement tests the teacher will want to select those that are most compatible with his goals. In addition to measurement, other types of evaluation are important in covering certain phases of the music program. Some individual testing may be desirable in spite of the time involved. Often, group measurement singles out those students who need to be evaluated individually.

NORMS

The final factor in usability is whether the test provides norms applicable to the local situation. The lack of such norms is a disadvantage, but it is not serious enough to rule out use of the test. Local norms can and should be established for tests that are to be used over a period of years, then both local and national norms considered in interpreting the test results.

VALIDITY

The most important consideration in selecting a test is whether or not it is valid. In the strict sense of the word, validity refers to the test results, that is, how closely the results mirror the real achievement of the class. Tests are always valid to some degree; validity is not an all-or-nothing condition, but a relative one. To the extent that a test is valid it can be helpful. A test with high validity measures what it says it measures. A test with low validity does not. When the test measures what it is designed to measure—aural skill, rhythm reading, knowledge of music symbols, or some other item—it is a valid test, but it must also be valid for the situation in which it is used and the purpose for which it was selected. This responsibility lies with the one who selects the test and not with the test designer. The user must know what it is he wants to measure, and he must know what the test can do. Often, the teacher, administrator, or researcher feels he is measuring one thing when he is really measuring something else.

Three kinds of validity are listed in the American Psychological Association (APA) publication, *Standards for Educational and Psychological Tests and Manuals:*[1] content validity, criterion-related validity, and construct validity.

CONTENT VALIDITY

Content validity is most important for the ordinary uses of achievement testing. It is concerned with how well the test represents the material actually taught, how well it takes into account different types of classrooms, different types of students, and different emphases upon the same basic material. Content validity is not determined solely on the basis of the material covered in a course; it is also related to the objectives of the course. One of the serious disadvantages of teacher-constructed tests is that they often cover only the material that has just been presented in the class; the frame of reference for the test is limited to the classroom for which it is designed. This is fair for determining whether the student has mastered the classroom material, but it gives no clue as to whether class time is being focused on the real goals of the course (although the two may be the same). A standardized test is an aid to teaching because it reflects broadly accepted content rather than a single teacher's selection and because it gives a measure of how students compare with a standard rather than only with their local peers.

Content validity is also based upon expert judgment. Experts who think broadly about the goals of music education are looked to as a major source for objectives. Logically, then, a test can have content validity if it has been constructed on the basis of what experts believe should be taught in music. Where the objectives and the evaluative tools are derived from the same source, the content validity should be high. (This is not an automatic good, for poor objectives may have been used making an inappropriate test.) Content validity involves more than the factual material or knowledge included in the objectives. It may also be concerned with the ways in which this material should be used by students. If the objectives state that the student should be able to list, to recognize, to define, to relate, then students should have opportunity in the test to list, to recognize, to define, and to relate. If the objectives include performance, the test should have some relationship to performance. Where

---

[1] John French and William Michael, cochairmen, *Standards for Educational and Psychological Tests and Manuals* (Washington, D.C.: American Psychological Association, Inc., 1966).

this is not possible, other forms of evaluation must be found for this area of the objectives. It is clear that objectives must be stated in terms that can be translated into evaluation; they must also be translatable into course content so that students know what they are learning and what they are being evaluated upon.

Content validity can also be established by adhering closely to a course outline, for the outline implies both the objectives and the content. Compared to those procedures previously mentioned, this method may be an easier way to establish content validity because behavioral objectives are often few in number and course content is often vague, but course outlines abound. Where agreement can be found among several course outlines and where the test corresponds to these, the test can be judged as having high content validity. Almost all carefully constructed published tests will have a statement concerning their content validity, what it is, and how it was determined. The prospective user of the test should look at this aspect carefully and should be very cautious when considering a test that does not provide evidence of content validity.

CRITERION-RELATED VALIDITY

To establish criterion-related validity, test scores are compared with a certain criterion related to the ability that the test measures. For example, if the test is a performance test designed to select the best high school instrumentalists, then the scores on this test should correlate highly with the selection of students for All State Band and Orchestra. A reasonably large percentage of students who made the higher scores on the test should be among those selected for All State performing groups, and there should be a lower percentage of students, perhaps none, selected for All State performing groups who made low scores on the test. Criterion-related validity, like other types of validity, is expressed in numerical terms. The numerical figure indicates the degree of correlation between the test and a criterion such as grades (1.00 being perfect correlation). Cronbach states that it is very unusual for a criterion-validity coefficient to rise above .60.[2] His examples show the coefficients for many excellent tests to be in the .40s and lower.

A test that helps to forecast how well a student will achieve in any one area, for example, college music theory, has predictive validity, a type of criterion-related validity. This differs from content validity in that the items used to predict may not actually relate to the content, though they usually do. One folktale long circulated was that long-fingered, slender

---

[2] Lee J. Cronbach, *Essentials of Psychological Testing*, 3rd ed. (New York: Harper & Row, Publishers, 1970), p. 135.

hands were the sign of artistic sensitivity. If this were indeed true, then one could use the shape of the hand as a predictor for artistic success, other things being equal. Predictive validity is of great importance in aptitude tests; how closely the aptitude scores agree with the student's true talent as evidenced by his later achievement indicates the criterion-related validity of the aptitude test. To establish such validity for an aptitude test, one could administer the test to a group of adults who have proven beyond a doubt that they are highly musical and to a second group of adults who have tried to master the elements of musicianship and failed. If the test is valid, the first group will score higher than the second group. The test would then be valid as a measure of musical talent in adults; any other conclusions that might be drawn about its efficiency in measuring aptitude in children or teenagers would be unverified. If the test were then given to grammar school students whose teachers had selected the most musical and the least musical in their classes, scores on the test should differentiate between these two groups also, if the test is valid for children.

Achievement tests are also concerned with predictive validity. The purpose of all measurement is to make decisions, and one proven way to decide who can achieve in a given area is on the basis of past achievement; for example, excellence in junior high music classes usually means ability to do well in senior high music classes. This type of prediction is a part of our common sense approach to selecting people for any pursuit: success in college is used as a predictor for success on the job; success in the job leads to further vocational opportunities. Although a test may not report predictive validity, it still may be very powerful in this respect. If a student has achieved, his chances for further achievement are good. The more comprehensive the test, the better the prediction can be. If a test has a predictive validity of .20, it will be better to use it than to make decisions entirely on a subjective or a chance basis.

Construct Validity

Construct validity has to do with how closely the test material matches a construct it purports to measure. A construct is defined as an idea or perception resulting from the orderly arrangement of facts; in music it may be considered a trait or an aspect of development. Music aptitude is the most familiar of the constructs in music; an aptitude test should yield high scores for those persons who show characteristics of high aptitude, who have, for example, well-developed performance skills, a high interest in music, a good musical memory, or similar traits. Scores from two aptitude tests should show a high correlation if both of them possess construct validity and are based on the same definition of aptitude.

Factor analysis is one method of identifying constructs for establishing construct validity. Easily accomplished with today's high-speed computers, factor analysis is a procedure that analyzes the results of a test and divides these results into factors that seem to be present. The computer identifies questions that contain a common factor, and the test maker or user must examine those questions carefully to determine what the common element is among them. Few music tests have been designed with much attention to construct validity, although factor analysis has been performed on some tests.

DETERMINING VALIDITY

In deciding whether a test has validity, content or any other kind, more must be inspected than the title of the test. Unless the content is scrutinized, the user may select a test in which all that is being evaluated is general intelligence or general musicality. These are important for learning, but a test should measure specifics upon which the teacher has spent instruction time. Validity is often expressed numerically, such as .80 or .96. This figure indicates the correlation between the score on the test and the score on some other evaluative tool that is considered a reliable and valid measure of the area for which the test is designed. A group test for auditory-visual skills might correlate .84 with scores for an individually administered sight-reading test. The criterion-related validity of the group test would then be expressed as .84. To obtain the validity of a new measure by comparing it with an established measure has both positive and negative value. A high validity is good if the new test has certain advantageous features not possessed by the older measure—has greater ease of administration or more scoring efficiency, is shorter or cheaper. On the other hand, if the two tests correlate too closely and are similar in other ways, the new one will simply be duplicating the older test and there will be little reason for its existence. Further, if the older test has not been satisfactory, a high correlation will mean that the new test shows little improvement over the other. Criterion-related validity can be determined for music tests by comparing test results with expert opinion. Care must be taken here to make sure the expert opinion is as objective as possible. This validity may also be established by comparing test results with the results from several other measurement tools. The use of several measures for comparison insures a broad basis for establishing any type of validity for a new test. At present, there are few means for determining a numerical validity coefficient for music tests, since few musical tasks have been accepted as definitive of valid musical achievement.

FACE VALIDITY

Face validity is a term found occasionally in the literature on testing. It is a meaningless term and should be abolished. It simply means that the test looks good, is printed by a reputable firm, was written by a well-established person, or some similar irrelevant and misleading fact. Face validity is no validity. No expert can casually look at a test and say with assurance that the test is a good measure of a certain area of learning. This is a compelling reason for the use of established, standardized tests in any teaching situation. The teacher-constructed test may look good and may have questions that test considerable knowledge or skill, but it may still be invalid for the purpose intended. To augment teacher-made tests and evaluative devices with a variety of standardized tests is to insure a balanced perspective for the teaching-learning situation.

SOURCES OF INVALIDITY

Invalidity has many causes, some not attributable to the test. Precision of language in the classroom is assumed by those who make standardized tests, but many teachers are imprecise or inconsistent about the use of musical terms. In their efforts to get the desired musical effect, teachers of performing groups will forget *crescendo, accelerando, tutti* and use *get louder, faster, now all together.* Students fail to learn the proper vocabulary and are unprepared for testing situations in which those terms are used. The test may then appear to be invalid when it is the teaching that lacks validity. Similarly, individual performance tests such as the *Watkins-Farnun Performance Scale* often cannot measure a student's performing ability because the student is unable to pick up the tempo from the metronome, one of the test's conditions. On the Watkins-Farnum scale, students who were unable to start have performed creditably when given a cue by the teacher. Since the teacher cue is a departure from the standardized procedure of the test, it lessens the validity of the test.

Tests may also be invalid for certain purposes when correlations are misinterpreted. For example, a high score on one of the published group tests in music reading does not insure that the student is proficient at reading music, because reading requires the additional motor skill of singing the precise pitch or fingering the correct pitch, skills not covered in group tests. However, a low score is a reliable indicator that the student cannot read music. Therefore, the user must be careful in interpreting the results accurately. This source of invalidity is present in most tests that provide information concerning what the student cannot do rather than what he can do. Music aptitude tests contain this same characteristic: high scores may not reliably predict high musical achievement because certain vital factors are not measured by the aptitude test, but low scores do indicate the doubtful possibility of musical achievement.

A source of invalidity in teacher-constructed tests and also in published tests is the wording of the instructions. This problem is partially avoided by questions in which musical stimuli form the answer choices or in which the student listens to select his answer rather than reading the answers. However, auditory questions that require subjective judgment can be poor. "Which is the better piece of music?" "Which interpretation is preferred?" There may be several correct answers to questions like these, depending upon the musical stimuli and the frame of reference. Questions that have unequivocal answers are always preferred, for where this is not possible, exact validity cannot be established.

Children can easily misunderstand questions, for they do not have the wealth of related background that the teacher uses to interpret the question and supply the answer. Students should not be exposed to ambiguous questions on tests or to obscure, overqualified statements in the classroom. The musician-teacher is often so concerned with exceptions to the rule that he never gives a clear-cut description of some musical item. The rules and statements given to children must be clear-cut and suited to their level; they must be qualified and amplified as the children grow in experience and understanding. The person who throws up his hands in horror when third graders are told that the Classical period used diatonic rather than chromatic melody is guilty of hewing to truth at the expense of learning. Dressel has pointed out that in the realm of affective objectives, extremes are both undesirable and ridiculous. As he says, "The person who becomes so imbued with sincerity and honesty that he cannot in any circumstance make a statement which has an element of untruth will not only become a terrible bore, but one of the most untactful individuals we can imagine."[3]

RELIABILITY

The third essential feature of a good evaluative device is reliability. Reliability is the element that indicates consistency in the taking of a

---

[3] Paul Dressel, "The Role of Evaluation in Teaching and Learning," *Evaluation in the Social Studies,* Thirty-fifth Yearbook of the National Council for the Social Studies, ed. Henry Berg (Washington, D.C.: National Council for the Social Studies, 1965), p. 12.

test. If a test is reliable and valid, an individual will obtain approximately the same scores when taking the test twice; his first score will be closely matched by his second score unless interim learning has focused upon the material covered in the test. A test is reliable when one can have confidence that the score it offers is an accurate statement of what one really knows about the questions asked. Music tests are often less reliable than tests in other fields; this may be because students learn so little in music that they are forced to guess a large percentage of the answers. Related to this is the tendency of teachers to avoid making music objective. No definite learning is presented, emphasized, and applied. In tests that have variety and a high level of difficulty and in which students are allowed to guess, reliability as reflected by class scores will be low because the guesses differ from day to day. Reliability in this instance can be improved by providing for "in doubt" responses. Excessive guessing should not be a reason for discarding the tests, but rather it should promote more frequent use of the tests to determine what portions of the material are not known.

Reliability in a test is a requirement for validity. If a test is not consistent in reporting, it cannot be valid. However, the degree of reliability necessary in a test is a matter of judgment. Leonhard and House[4] suggest the following guidelines:

Reliability

.85–.99   high to very high; valuable for individual measurement and diagnosis

.80–.84   fairly high; some value in individual measurement and highly satisfactory in group measurement

.70–.79   rather low; adequate for group measurement; of doubtful value in individual measurement

.50–.69   low; inadequate for individual measurement, but of some value in group measurement

below .50   very low; inadequate for use

These figures offer a guideline but are probably high. They are appropriate for standardized tests in the cognitive and skill areas, but are unrealistically high when considering evaluative tools developed by the teacher. They also would not apply to devices for measurement in the affective domain, because this is an area for which little is known about testing. The average classroom-developed test seldom has a reliability above .60–.70. The purpose of the test has much bearing upon the im-

---

[4] Charles Leonhard and Robert House, *Foundations and Principles of Music Education* (New York: McGraw-Hill Book Company, 1959), p. 341.

portance of reliability. If the test is used primarily as a learning device, reliability need not be critical. If the test is to measure overall achievement or to determine how closely the goals of the program are being met, its reliability becomes important. If the purpose of the test is placement, to determine who should study music and who should not, who should be encouraged and who discouraged, then the test should be as reliable as possible. Aptitude tests that are given only once and for which no background of achievement is felt to be necessary should have reliabilities as high as possible—above .90 or .95.

Other factors in test selection or construction may override the matter of reliability. (1) Where the situation makes use of many evaluative devices, a lower reliability can be accepted if one of the types of validity is well established. (2) Frequent testing and measurement will also compensate for decision errors due to low reliability. (3) The content of the test is a factor in determining the importance of the reliability. A low reliability of significant relationships is more informative than high reliability with test questions that are trivial in nature. Negative illustrations of this point can be found in doctoral dissertations that are concerned, at least partially, with the problem of preparing evaluative tools; frequently, more attention is given to the arithmetical figure that indicates the reliability of the question than to the content of the question. As a result, test items are discarded on this arithmetical criterion, resulting in a loss of valuable information and a retention of unimportant but reliable data. When using evaluation for research or teaching, thought is far more important than all the rules and formulas devised by statisticians.

RELIABILITY COEFFICIENT

The reliability coefficient is a numerical indication of how consistent a test would be were it given to all students under all testing conditions. Most reliability figures are computed on an internal consistency basis; that is, the test is measured against itself to determine whether it is consistent or not. Items are compared upon computer-based analyses, or some process is used to divide the test into two equal halves so that results on the two halves can be compared. This latter process is often referred to as the split-half method. Test questions are divided by odd and even numbers, by random selection, or the first half of the test against the second half where the questions are assigned to the test in a random order of difficulty. If the scores on each half are approximately the same, if they equal or match each other closely, the reliability is high. However, where reliability is computed on only half the test, reliability is lower because less accuracy is possible when there are fewer items. Total reliability must then be estimated. The addition of more items increases the reliability of any test, everything else being equal.

Besides the split-half method, other methods used for computing reliability are the test-retest and the equivalent forms test. In the test-retest, the identical test is given a second time and the two scores compared for consistency. Obvious disadvantages exist for this method with achievement tests: where the test is of such nature that the questions can be retained or the questions follow a discernible pattern, these facts will be applied to the retest situation and the scores measurably increased. The reliability will then appear low. If too long a period elapses between the test and the retest, conditions such as maturation or additional learning will change the retest score and lower the reliability. The exact length of time between the two administrations for determining reliability will depend upon the nature of the test. With most music aptitude tests there would be little carry-over, so the retest could probably follow the test promptly with little retention occurring. For an achievement test based upon factual knowledge, prompt retesting would probably not be satisfactory, because some test items would be retained. The success of the equivalent forms methods for establishing reliability depends upon how nearly identical in difficulty and constructs are the two forms of the test. If they are truly identical, this method for establishing reliability would be the most accurate. One form could be given one day, the other version soon after, and the results used to compute reliability. However, it is very difficult to construct two tests that are exactly equivalent; in music, only three published tests claim to have two equivalent forms, and these have not been subjected to sufficiently rigorous scrutiny to determine whether the forms actually do equal each other.

The homogeneity of a test affects its reliability. When all of the items are similar, one can expect higher reliability. Where the test is made up of several sections each measuring a different skill, the reasonable expectation is that some students will do better on some sections than on others. Because reliability is computed on the basis of internal consistency, this variation in scores between test sections will lower the reliability of the test. However, a test measuring several related skills can be acceptable with a lower reliability if each subsection is relatively reliable and the content is valid. The additional information to be gained from such a test is of two kinds: the subpart scores offer information as to specific achievement, and the total score reflects a combination of abilities, highly desirable in evaluating musical progress. For diagnostic work, the homogeneous test that can identify specific weaknesses of a student is helpful, but for general measurement the heterogeneous test is very useful even with lower reliability.

Reliability can be affected by instructions and by scoring. Unless the teacher is careful, his instructions may vary noticeably from one class to the next. One period he is very explicit, the next brief. The scores reflect this difference and lower the reliability. Similarly in scoring, the teacher's or evaluator's reaction may change and affect his objectivity. The test that can be machine scored or hand marked using a template is superior in this respect to a performance test or an essay test in which the adjudicator must maintain a stable basis for judgment. Contest judges are accustomed to accusations of unfairness, because the large number of performances and the pressure of the time schedule warp their objectivity. They are influenced by the performance that preceded, by their increasing familiarity with the task, by the fifth repetition of a number that should never have been allowed to be a contest selection, by fatigue, by boredom with the same kind of errors over and over, and by the live distractions of the contest situation. Reports of high reliability in such situations should be accepted with skepticism, for the evaluator who can maintain a highly reliable rating is probably influenced by nonessential constants, such as the type of number or appearance of the individual. For contest situations, a reliability above .75 should be considered satisfactory. Too many stories are told about English themes being given A grades one day and D grades the next by the same reader to believe that in a music contest there could not be similar fluctuation. Computers are now being programed to grade essay papers; perhaps the day may come when computers will judge music contests and the problem of subjective judgment will be overcome at last.

Standardized tests reduce these sources of unreliability by providing very specific directions for administering and scoring the test. Competent teachers must know that such directions are to be followed exactly if the test results are to be meaningful. Additional explanations may aid some students but confuse others, and are sure to decrease the usability of the norms. Use of a phonograph record or tape helps insure greater uniformity of directions and of the testing situation itself, but makes it necessary for all students to stay with the record. For the slower-paced individual, this creates some of the aspects of a speed test and forces guessing, thus lowering the reliability. In tests where each item on the record is not given a number (the Seashore, for example), students can become confused and begin marking the inappropriate question, again lowering the reliability.

The statement has already been made that a test should be neither selected nor rejected solely on the basis of reliability. A difficult test may offer relatively low reliability, but the test author and the teacher may feel the material to be of importance and to require evaluation. As students increase their ability in this difficult area, the reliability of the test may be expected to rise. Often this can be verified by noting that the test reliability increases with age level. If an achivement test is compatible with course objectives and has adequate reliability for older, more knowledgeable students, there is no reason to reject it as a learning device for the younger level.

In general, the longer the test the more reliable. If the test must fit into a twenty-minute period, it will tend to be less reliable than a test of one hour's length. Length does not influence reliability where the items are all so easy that most of the students answer them correctly, or where the items are so difficult that a high percentage of students miss all the answers. Reliability is improved when there is a wide spread to the test items—some easy, some difficult, some in between—for it can accommodate a wide range of achievers and produce a wide spread in test results.

The test that is designed to cover too broad an area of achievement will be unreliable. In an effort to evaluate all the possible learnings of a high school performing group, tests have been constructed that contain only one or two questions on each area of musical knowledge or skill. The reliability of such a test is spurious in terms of content because reliability cannot be established on the basis of a single question here and there. Reliability figures for this type of test indicate consistency in what is common to the standardization group, and not anything about the test itself.

The teacher must combine the realities of the situation with idealism. Knowing that music tests may have lower reliabilities due to uneven motivation, questionable testing conditions, and a feeling among the students that testing is not too important, the teacher must balance this knowledge with the need for objectivity and information in decisions about learning. Written tests are more reliable than oral quizzes where bad sampling, subjective judgment, unstandardized procedures, uneven wording, and other flaws mar the evaluative situation.

USEFULNESS

A test may be reliable, valid, and usable, but it must also be useful. Since the purpose of a test is the improvement of the teaching-learning process, the test must contribute to this if it is to be useful. Easy tests can be constructed so that all those being tested can obtain a high score—they have the required skill or knowledge—and thus the test will be reliable; it may measure what it is supposed to and thus be valid; it may be quick and easy to score and thus be usable. However, if it tests the results of maturation and fails to test learned material or to discriminate good students from poor, it is not useful in terms of improving instruction. The reader of doctoral dissertations can find reports of music tests in which 70 percent of the students made perfect scores; for many such tests one may suspect that nonmusic students could score nearly as high as the musicians. Such tests are not useful because they do not differentiate.

THE SITUATION FOR TESTING

Testing, whether with standardized or teacher-constructed devices, requires special attention to the situation. There are several conditions that must be observed if the measurement is to fulfill its purpose. The first of these is that students and administrators must know the purpose of the tests and, if possible, be involved in planning and preparing for the test. Student involvement is always wise for any kind of test. When a test is used as a threat in order to motivate students to achievement, it may serve its purpose but have unwanted side effects. Students will soon realize the intent of the testing and acquire negative attitudes toward the course, the teacher, and the test. A final test, one given at the end of the course, may be useful in measuring the year's achievement but offer little to the student in the way of guidance for further learning; the opportunities to repair deficiencies are past for the year. The best use of a test is to provide information to student and teacher on progress in various aspects of learning and achievement. If students are well informed, if they have discussed the type of test and its purposes, positive motivation will take place both before and after the test.

The second condition for good testing is that students must have the opportunity to do their best. Often, the testing situation is less reliable and valid than the test itself. Unconscious hints are given that benefit some students but are meaningless to others; distractors are present that affect some students more than others. One student is affected by the sound of a fire engine outside and loses his train of thought; another is distracted by the structure of the question or by a misspelled word and thinks about this rather than about the question; some students are aided by responses to questions asked during the test; extra time is allowed the last few students in the room at the end of the period, or they may be given additional help or pressured to leave. The scheduling of the test may militate against high achievement; it may be planned for the day after the school play or the morning of the year's biggest football game, affecting some students but not others. On the other hand, it is equally important to avoid making the test of too great consequence. It should be treated primarily as another learning experience, one for which preparation is made, but not accompanied by locked doors, hushed atmosphere, and whispering teacher. Admittedly, the test situation is a contrived one; however, the performing situation is also contrived, and both students and teachers adjust to this fact. The student who has learned how to do his best in the testing situation gives both himself and the teacher a more accurate guide to his progress, for his test score is not influenced by nervousness, inability to remember things he knows under normal conditions, or a sense of great pressure.

The third consideration is that the testing situation must be identical for each student. The use of phonograph records for tests is often questioned because the audio output is quite different from school to school, even from room to room; the better the machine, the better the record will be for the testing situation. Poor fidelity is a factor in listening tests that demand great acuity, such as the Seashore measures. In most achievement tests, the quality of sound may not affect the validity of a test item, but the student could be affected by added distractors so that the reliability suffers. Oral questions and answers typical of the classroom situation are of great learning value but are not acceptable as objective measurement because the situation cannot be duplicated. For each student the situation is different, influenced by the questions and answers that have preceded. Similarly, oral questions for which students write replies are not acceptable, because the teacher cannot duplicate the exact conditions from class to class or even in the same class if the questions are given at different times. This kind of quiz is useful in evaluation, but it is not measurement. Another type of tool is the written test in which students are allowed to choose two out of three questions to answer. Because this is not identical for all students, it is only an evaluation device and not a test.

The oral examination is usually unstructured, without even a written record of it. In addition, responses in an oral examination are affected by the audience present. Oral quizzes, or even the kind of intensive oral examination typical of graduate degrees, are best when used after written measures have offered a controlled and accurate evaluation. The oral quiz may show how able the student is in verbal clarity or may probe some special area more deeply than the written measures. Similarly, with informal performance in the classroom, where the teacher calls occasionally upon one or two students to demonstrate or play a passage, it is impossible to be objective. No adequate sample is obtained, certain players or sections are called upon more frequently than others—

those that are consistently good or consistently bad are usually singled out—and the tasks they are asked to perform vary in difficulty. Neither is the observer consistent; after three students in a row have missed a rhythmic pattern, the teacher's objectivity decreases. Individual performance, like oral quizzes, is a good evaluative tool and a good learning device, but it fails to meet the third consideration for good testing, that the situation be identical for each student.

The essay test is another example of a tool for which standardization is needed in scoring. Essay tests have much value, since they help the student learn to make connections between events and items, to generalize, to fit pertinent details into the broad picture, and to transfer knowledge from one area to another. They also help the student learn to express himself in writing, a useful skill for any adult. However, the essay offers many pitfalls in the path toward objectivity. Writing skill can hide ignorance, and awkward writing can disguise a knowledgeable answer. Essay tests should be scored anonymously and one question at a time; the first question should be scored on every test paper before the second question is examined. There are at least two ways to introduce some objectivity into the process of reading an essay answer. In the analytical method, the teacher writes out the complete correct answer and assigns points to every part of the answer. The student's answer is then compared with the model answer, and he receives points for the parts he included. Points are subtracted for errors in his answer. All extra ideas and items in the answer, no matter how insightful or correct, are ignored. The second method is a rating method in which each question is rated on a five- or seven-point scale such as very good, good, adequate, and so on. The composite grade is the sum of the numerical ratings on the individual questions. This method is faster than the analytical method, but it is not as reliable. Essay questions and the model answers must be precise, or else the student is justified in interpreting the question in the way he can answer it best. A question such as "Trace the breakdown of the tonal system," or "Show how Bach and Handel are the culmination of the Baroque period," are so all-encompassing that many types of answers that can be deemed adequate will fail to answer the points the question writer had in mind.

A fourth condition for successful testing is that the test must be given at the appropriate time. The purpose of the test given at the end of the course is different from that of tests used as the course progresses. A different type of mastery is expected at the end of the year from that measured during the course—a broader understanding of factual material, a more musical interpretation in performance, or a greater insight into formal structure when listening. In the middle of the learning period, testing may often focus upon details, but a final measurement will probably be more concerned with ability to relate and to see the whole picture. Some measurements are used to determine what students retain after a period of time has elapsed; here again, the purpose must determine both the nature of the test and the time it is to be given. For example, in examining the effect that missing academic classes for instrumental instruction may have on academic achievement, it would be unreasonable to test after the summer vacation period. In the intervening months, both the academic learning and the musical learning may have faded so greatly that the testing will be unable to produce any results. On the other hand, if retention of academic or musical learning over the vacation period is of interest, the test results may be quite meaningful.

The more the teacher knows, the better will be the students' progress. The teacher must know the material; he must also know about teaching methods and their appropriate uses, and he must know about testing and measurement. The statement has been made that music teachers must be better trained before they will be able to use tests successfully, whether tests of their own construction or published measures. Unfortunately, the statement is true. Music teachers have little contact with measurement in their college and graduate preparation, so they are wary of using already-existing tests and are even more reluctant to construct their own. Use of ready-made devices is a more natural step towards an evaluation program for music education than is the widespread use of teacher constructed tests. Use of published, standardized tests will also affect a greater change in achievement than will teacher-constructed tests.

The test administrator is not always the teacher. The school psychologist, the guidance counselor, or the music supervisor may assume responsibility for administering a standardized test, though rarely for a teacher-constructed test. In the past, there has been concern among the testing profession that qualified people administer tests, because the teacher was not competent or sophisticated enough. Hopefully, enough criticism of this view has been voiced that the teacher will be given the responsibility. If he can be trusted to teach the great ideas of the world, he can surely be trusted to interpret a standardized test. A better testing situation occurs when the teacher is in charge, for the student can identify with him, rapport is established, and the teacher may know how to interpret any nonroutine reaction from a student. In addition, a more serious effort will be made by students, for they understand that the test is an important part of the classwork. However, the teacher who is not interested or is antagonistic toward the test will be a negative factor, for student performance will reflect his attitude. In order to increase his understanding, the teacher should take the test himself before administering it to students. When this is done, many criticisms of inept teacher administration can be avoided.

THE LIMITATIONS OF TESTING

Measurement is probably the best single avenue to improved musical instruction in the public schools. This has been sufficiently stressed in the preceding pages and chapters. There are, however, limitations to the contribution that testing can make.

First, it is impossible to adequately test all areas of music learning. Music has already been described as including the cognitive, psychomotor, and affective domains; it covers listening skills, aural skills, performance skills, knowledge of score reading, knowledge of history, and knowledge of aesthetic principles.

Second, tests may be limited in their spread of difficulty. Some tests are designed to be of even difficulty, some of varying difficulty. Each has its advantages. The comprehensive test should be of varying difficulty to provide discrimination, to give students confidence, to obtain information concerning the most able students. The daily test may be of even difficulty because it centers on one objective and its purpose is to determine if that objective has been mastered. The teacher may desire several questions of about equal difficulty to give a fair picture of progress toward the goal. The daily test is usually teacher-constructed, and writing a homogeneous test takes some experience, or at least careful thought. A major drawback in the classroom test is that it is hastily constructed; the teacher hurries home from a concert to prepare a test for the next day's class. Small wonder that little faith is put in the testing process.

Third, tests are not adaptable. When tests are given to a different type of group from that used for the standardization, comparison with the national norms may be meaningless. The local scores can then be compared only with each other and one advantage of the standardized test will be lost. This kind of problem can be diminished if the test users are knowledgeable and careful. Selection of the test, the use made of it, and methods of administering it and interpreting it can increase the adaptability of a test and broaden its usefulness. When carefully used, even inaccurate measures have value. A test can augment or complete teacher judgment, or it may contradict teacher judgment, in which case the knowledge of the teacher and the quality of the test become crucial.

Problems in the improvement of measurement can be solved by educating both music teachers and professional educators as to what music tests can and cannot do. Music teachers must give more stress to the content of music, and to student achievement in the content, if they wish music to achieve equal status with English or biology. A sound testing program is essential if content is to be stressed. If the teacher is too busy to give standardized tests or to construct good tests of his own, he needs to re-examine the nature of his objectives and activities to see what is really being accomplished in his music program.

QUESTIONS FOR DISCUSSION

1. In addition to the sample items mentioned in the text, what additional conditions affect the reliability, validity, and usefulness of music tests?
2. Inspect several aptitude tests and several achievement tests and determine the type of validity reported.
3. Construct a checklist of items to look for in selecting tests for classroom use. Identify each as being essential, very important, or desirable. Answers may be checked against the APA monograph on test standards.
4. What evidence is acceptable for criterion-related validity for aptitude tests?
5. What constructs comprise musicality?
6. From an examination of music tests, select those that seem to be most acceptable for music instruction based on the discussion in this chapter.

REFERENCES

Ahmann, J. Stanley, and Marvin Glock, *Evaluating Pupil Growth* (2nd ed.). Boston: Allyn and Bacon, Inc., 1963, Part III.

Anastasi, Anne, *Psychological Testing* (3rd ed.). New York: The Macmillan Company, 1968, Chapters 4–6.

Cronbach, Lee J., *Essentials of Psychological Testing* (3rd ed.). New York: Harper & Row, Publishers, 1970, Chapters 5–6.

French, John, and William Michael, cochairmen, *Standards for Educational and Psychological Tests and Manuals*. Washington, D.C.: American Psychological Association, Inc., 1966.

Gronlund, Norman, *Measurement and Evaluation in Teaching*. New York: The Macmillan Company, 1965, Chapter 13.

Lundin, Robert W., *An Objective Psychology of Music* (2nd ed.). New York: The Ronald Press Company, 1967, Chapter 12.

Shuter, Rosamund, *The Psychology of Musical Ability*. London: Methuen & Co. Ltd., 1968, Part I.

Stanley, Julian, *Measurement in Today's Schools* (4th ed.). Englewood Cliffs, N.J.: Prentice-Hall, Inc., 1964, Chapter 5.

CHAPTER THREE

interpreting the results of evaluation

The most important aspect of evaluation is the use made of the results. The results must be interpreted correctly; the characteristics of the test or other evaluative tool should be thoroughly understood, and any statistical data provided must be meaningful to the user. After a tool has been selected and administered, the teacher must use sound judgment in determining the meaning of the resulting scores.

The more knowledgeable the teacher, the more effective his use of the information derived from evaluation. The purpose of this chapter is to present an understanding of terms such as measures of central tendency, frequency distribution, correlation, standard score, standard error, chance scores, and item analysis. The foundation for these discussions is the score itself and the normal curve that is the usual pattern for a large group of scores.

NORMAL CURVE AND SCORE

In emphasizing exactitude in administering, scoring, and interpreting tests, the erroneous impression is often given that the *score* itself is of unswerving, exact significance. Quite the contrary. Test scores do not prove anything; they should be thought of as reflecting ability, not determining it. Test scores suggest, together with all other relevant information, a pattern of achievement that the teacher must interpret, using a happy balance between objectivity and insight. Scores are not exact points on a scale but are indicators of the student's true score. Often, bands are used on either side of the score to indicate that the true score is probably somewhere between two numerical points.

A test score, such as 50 or 80, does not have any meaning except in relation to the other scores achieved on the same test. A score of 80 cannot be interpreted numerically; it is better than a score of 40, but how much better depends on several factors. Teacher-constructed tests are often interpreted on a basis of: below 70, failing; between 71 and 92, average; 93 or above, superior. This practice is unfair for several reasons. First, teacher-made tests are inconsistent; second, an unexpected spread of scores may occur that changes the relative meaning of the scores; and third, teachers often fail to ask questions that reflect the expected learnings and the stated goals. When the grade interpretation cited above seems to be fair, what may have happened is that the teacher, consciously or unconsciously, has taught for the test during the class meetings previous to the test or that the test is based upon what the students seemed to be learning just prior to the test. When the teacher uses such a grading system, he fails to discriminate between those who have learned and those who have not. If most of the students make grades in the 80s and 90s, the teacher is probably satisfied that he has taught them all well. From the elementary school right through the university, the same approach to grading may be seen in music—the predominance of A's and B's, with C the normal bottom of the grading scale and D awarded only to the incorrigibles. What saves the university music program is a strict entrance system, which establishes a relatively high standard of skill and knowledge. The self-confidence of many unmusical and badly trained individuals who come expecting entrance into a school of music is indicative that they have been encouraged and rewarded for their efforts in the public schools. Neither the grades they have received nor the tests they have taken have opened their eyes to the need for more achievement, more improvement, and greater understanding.

If the 70 to 100 method of grading is not valid, the teacher must have some other frame of reference by which to determine that the students are learning and what they are learning. When evaluative tools are based upon some point system other than 100, or when a tool is used that is not a test and follows a different method of scoring, the teacher must have a frame of reference by which to interpret the scores.

Chance scores must also be considered. A chance score is one that could be made purely by guessing, without actually knowing any of the material. With a two-choice answer—same and different, yes and no, higher and lower—students can guess and obtain a score of 50 percent by chance. When norms for a published test show a chance score to be respectable, the test is providing very little information, if any. The chance score does not always mean that the student knows nothing about the material, but this is a possibility. Several published music tests have norms that rate chance scores relatively high. These tests, promoted by instrument manufacturing companies, are characterized by two-choice answers and high chance scores. In addition, the norms given with such tests have no basis in fact. The purpose of such tools is to insure that no students will be discouraged, that all students will score at least *fair* or above. These norms therefore provide no interpretive data and little predictive value.

When guessing is not desired and there is a need to determine how much guessing is involved, the *correction for guessing formula* can be used as a deterrent. Errors are given greater weight than omissions, so the student is penalized more for a wrong answer than for a blank. This procedure seldom changes the relative standing of students, but it may enhance the meaningfulness of the raw scores. At present there are no music tests that recommend use of correction for guessing formulas.

The *normal curve* (standard curve or normal distribution) is a picture of the distribution of scores. The curve is based on the assumption that when a large number of random scores are available they fall into a pattern that always has the same shape. A surprisingly large number of items involving human traits and behavior follow a distribution closely approximating a normal curve. This is not a single curve that fits all tests or all characteristics, but rather a family of curves. The normal distribution assumes that more students will obtain the average or mean score than any other one score. This is seen as the high point appearing in the middle of the curve. The high part of the curve represents the largest number of students.

In Figure 1, each normal curve has the same mean, or average, and the same number of students, but the distribution or range of scores differs. In a knowledge test, the normal distribution might be expected to look like curve A with many students obtaining nearly the same score (assuming all had been well taught and had learned the material as well as their ability allowed). With musical talent, the curve might resemble curve B with a wider distribution and fewer students grouped together in the middle. In curve A most of the students might have scored within three or four points on either side of the mean, while in curve B the same percentage of students may have scores fifteen points on either side of the mean. Curve C represents a still wider distribution. In Figure 2, the different normal curves represent different-sized groups, the highest curve representing the largest number.

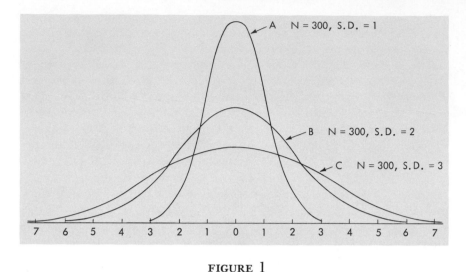

FIGURE 1

sent different-sized groups, the highest curve representing the largest number.

Teachers often misunderstand the normal distribution and attempt to grade "on the curve" for a small group of students. It is seldom wise to force a group of fifteen or twenty scores into a normal curve, because the sample is too small to be considered random or representative of a true cross section. *Parametric statistics* is the name given to statistics that assume normal distribution, and this kind of statistical treatment is rarely used for small groups.

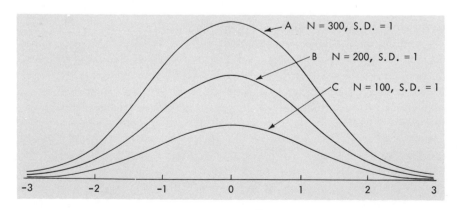

FIGURE 2

MEASURES OF CENTRAL TENDENCY

Groups are usually described in terms of what is average or expected. Those who excel are those who deviate markedly from the group upwards, and those who fail deviate markedly downwards from the group. Emphasis is placed upon finding the central tendency or central point of any group. In evaluation, the following types of central tendency are the most common.

MEAN

The *mean* score, often written as $\overline{X}$, is the average score of the group being considered. The mean score is easily computed by adding all of the scores and dividing this sum by the number of scores used. It has at least two advantages: it is easily understood, and it is easily obtained by a process everyone has mastered. It should always be used as a measure of central tendency unless there is a good reason not to, such as where the scores are badly skewed or truncated.

MODE

The *mode* is another measure of central tendency sometimes used in evaluation. It is often called the crude mode because it is not an accurate measure, particularly where small groups are concerned. The mode is the score made by the most students. For example, if there are five students in a class, one scoring 87, two scoring 53, one 52, and one 51, the mode would be 53. However, if one of the students scoring 53 had instead scored 87, the mode then would be 87, radically changing the measure of central tendency. In the symmetrical normal curve, the mode and the mean are the same, for the peak of the curve indicates quantity as well as midpoint. In these instances, usual with large groups, the mode is a satisfactory indicator of central tendency. The advantage of the mode is that it is simple to compute; one has only to find the score achieved by the most students. However, its value is so limited that it is mentioned here primarily to give familiarity with the term.

MEDIAN

The *median* is helpful in interpreting scores and is the measure of central tendency whenever percentiles are involved. Where schools

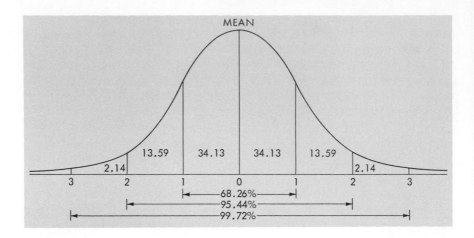

have recorded only the percentiles (norms) for a standardized test taken by various classes, the differences in class sizes make use of the mean impossible; therefore, the median must be used to determine the average achievement. The median is the middlemost point and is obtained by arranging all scores (or percentiles) in a rank order, from top to bottom, then finding the exact middle. Where there is an odd number of scores, the median will be the middle score; for example, where there are thirty-one scores the sixteenth score up from the bottom would also be the sixteenth score down from the top. Where there is an even number of scores, the median will lie halfway between the two middle scores; for example, where there are thirty scores, the median will be halfway between the fifteenth and sixteenth scores. The process of finding the median is made more complicated where the scores are available only by grouped distribution, such as five students scoring between 90 and 95, twelve scoring between 80 and 90, and so on. The median will then fall within a group of scores, and the exact numerical figure must be computed by an algebraic formula. For this formula, reference may be made to any text on measurement.

The median is also useful when there are extreme scores in the group that exert excessive influence upon the mean. A good example is that of annual income for four teachers living in one block. Teacher 1 earns $7000, Teacher 2 earns $8500, Teacher 3 $9500, and Teacher 4 has inherited 2 million dollars, the interest on which brings his annual income to $109,000. The mean for this group would be over $33,700, not a very good indication of the income for the average teacher in that block. However, the median would be the point halfway between the two middle figures, or $9050, a much better approximation of an average teacher salary. Where figures for a music test are similarly skewed by the inclusion of scores for an exceptional group—for example, a group of students with perfect pitch taking an aural test—the median is a more appropriate measure of central tendency than the mean. In a small class, one or two irresponsible students can lower the mean unrealistically, or an exceptionally talented and well-trained student may make it too high, and here again the median is useful. When national norms are used, the mean is the better measure, because the extremes have been included in the norming sample.

MEASURES OF DISPERSION

STANDARD DEVIATION

How far away from the mean or center of a normal curve can a score be, and still be considered somewhat average? The following diagram illustrates the manner in which *standard deviation* divides test scores that are normally distributed. One standard deviation away from the mean encompasses approximately 34 percent of the population, so about 68 percent of the total lies within one standard deviation on either side of the mean. The second standard deviation above and below the mean will include another 13.5 percent, for a total of 27 percent, with 95.5 percent of all scores within two standard deviations. The third standard deviation above and below the mean includes 2 percent of the population, and combined is slightly more than 4 percent. The total of these percentages does not quite equal 100; in a large sample, there are always extremes that fall outside the normal curve. In the diagram, the curved line never touches the bottom line, thus allowing for extremes. By determining where a student's score or a class mean is with relation to the *normal,* one can obtain some idea of the meaning of the score. The value of one standard deviation, in scoring points, should be reported by the publisher in a standardized test. A teacher can approximate this for his own tests by using the percentages to obtain an indication of spread. For example, one published test has a standard deviation of approximately ten points with fourth-grade students. The average score on the national norms is about forty-four from a possible eighty-three points. Approximately 68 percent of the fourth-grade students taking this test will score between 34 and 54, one standard deviation either side of the mean of 44.

Standard deviation is affected by the distribution of scores within the class, and this is usually related to the number of questions. Where a test has a large number of questions or items, the spread of scores and hence the standard deviation will usually be greater than where the number of test questions is more limited. Standard deviation, then, is a measure of the spread of the scores, giving some meaning to the scores in relationship to the performance of the total population.

RANGE

The *range of scores,* as was indicated earlier, can be helpful in understanding test scores and interpreting the mean and the median. There is value in knowing that, in addition to having a mean score of 80, the class range was from 12 to 98. In view of the high average, the teacher would want to take a second look at the paper of someone scoring 12. The possibility of an error in scoring is always present, or the individual making the score of 12 might be faced with problems for which some help can be found. A second consideration where one or more low scores occur and the average is high is that the scores are bunched together in the low 90s for a 100-point test, and the test is providing very little discrimination except for the extremes. The total range is relatively crude and unstable and is affected by one unusually high or unusually low score.

DECILE RANGE AND QUARTILE RANGE

At least two procedures may be used to counteract the effect just described. The most useful indication of central tendency with range of scores is a *decile range* where the top and bottom 10 percent of the scores are dropped and the range of the middle 80 percent is considered.

The second procedure is to divide the total range of scores into *quartiles.* Quartiles are points on the rating scale that divide test scores into quarters: Q1 (quartile 1) is at the 25th percentage point from the bottom, Q2 at the median, and Q3 at the 75th percentile. When a standardized test mentions the quartile range, the term refers to the range of scores encompassing 25 percent of the students; interquartile range is the middle 50 percent, those 25 percent on either side of Q2— that is, the scores ranging from the 25th percentile to the 75th percentile.

CORRELATION

A *correlation* is a relationship. Correlations are of great importance for a test, because the value of the test lies in the relationship it posses-ses to various kinds of achievement or aptitude. A discussion of correlation would be easier if a certain point could be established at which one could say, "Above this, correlations are meaningful for certain purposes; below this point, correlations might indicate a discrepancy; whether high or low, correlations provide valuable information." Unfortunately, high and low correlations are like good and bad Schumann—compared with Brahms or with Mendelssohn, the songs, the piano music, or the orchestral works? What is good and most meaningful depends upon the comparison and upon the situation.

Correlations are shown numerically, on a 201-point scale (from −1.00 to +1.00). A correlation coefficient of 1.00 would be perfect, zero or .00 would show complete absence of relationship. Correlations can be negative as well as positive. In the famous experiment, if the dog salivated every time the bell rang, the correlation would be +1.00, a perfect positive correlation. If the dog never salivated when the bell was rung, the correlation would be −1.00, a perfect negative correlation. If the dog salivated half the time and failed to do so half the time, there would be no relationship between the two and the correlation would be .00. However, correlation is not evidence of causation, because a third factor may be present. If, each time the bell rings, a bone drops in front of the dog and he salivates, one does not know whether it is the bell or the bone that brings about the salivating. Common sense may indicate it is the bone. Thus, correlation is not necessarily a sign of cause and effect. Educational situations are rarely as clear cut as this example, and the factors in any situation that help to bring about a correlation may be hard to detect. Stanley gives a good example of confusion between correlation and causation.

> Going to Sunday school is generally believed to be valuable from many standpoints, but a positive relationship between the rate of attendance and characteristics such as honesty does not *necessarily* imply that children are honest because they attend Sunday School. Underlying and causing both attendance and honesty may be home training, for example. A really crucial test of the hypothesis that attending Sunday School makes children more honest would have to be experimental rather than correlational.[2]

A second fact to keep in mind about correlations is that they do not always work both ways. A study to determine the relationship between musicality and intelligence would establish that the correlation betwcen musicality and I.Q. scores is high. However, to reverse the state-

---

[2] Julian C. Stanley, *Measurement in Today's School*, 4th ed. (Englewood Cliffs, N.J.: Prentice-Hall, Inc., 1964), p. 91.

ment and say that the correlation between intelligence and musicality is high would not have the same validity. The researcher who starts with a group of intelligent people to determine whether they are also musical has a different set of data from what he would have if he started with musical people to determine whether they are intelligent. This carelessness has resulted in much wasted discussion and poor conclusions in music research. It is like saying that a cow is an animal that eats grass, therefore an animal that eats grass is a cow. Stanley adds to his illustration, "Would it be logical to assume that children attend Sunday school because they are honest?"

INTERPRETING THE TEST

PERCENTILES

Percentiles are the accepted method for presenting test norms. The percentile figure for a score indicates where that score stands in relation to all the other scores on a percentage basis, hence the name percentile. A score that is at the 99th percentile does not mean the student missed only one out of a hundred, but that 99 percent of the scores on the test were lower than his. Hence, a score that appears to be only moderately high may rank at the 98th or 99th percentile if the test is of such difficulty that few or no scores are higher. Percentiles have the disadvantage that one cannot add them up and divide by the number of tests to obtain a final rating for a course. If all the subtests are weighted equally, such a procedure will be fairly accurate, but not precise enough for most evaluation purposes. Percentile points, like scores, can be misleading since the student's true score lies within a range on either side of the given percentile rather than at that exact point. The use of percentile bands is therefore recommended in interpreting test scores to students. The band is often one standard error of measurement[1] on either side of the point score achieved. To understand percentile, one should keep in mind that at the extreme ends of the percentile range, as one goes farther in either direction from the midpoint, the same size percentile band will include a wider range of scores than close to the midpoint. In other words, the difference of ten percentile points from the 45th to the 55th percentile might indicate a difference of eight points

---

[1] For a definition, see page 61.

on the test, but to move from the 85th to the 95th percentile, again a difference of ten percentile points, might require a score that is twenty-five to thirty points higher.

RANK

A method of looking at scores without reference to norms is to *rank* them: John first in the class, Mary second, and Rosemary the lowest. The British advocate this as a reasonable approach to music contests and performance because it is realistic—only one performer at the professional level is chosen concert master or soprano soloist. Competition does not allow for two equally capable individuals to be employed for one position. This type of ranking may at times be more helpful to teacher and student than the commonly used ratings of superior, excellent, good, fair, and poor. Rank position has only informal value, however, because it is affected by the size of the group. Ranking third in a class of 600 probably indicates a more significant achievement than third in a class of 100, though this is not always true. Percentile rank is superior to ranking of raw scores because it tends to equalize the effect of class size. Thus, a student who ranks 33rd out of 100 students would have the same percentile rank as the student who is 3rd out of a class of 10.

STANDARD SCORES

Standard scores are provided for most standardized tests. These are usually nearly the same relative score as the percentile score. For most purposes, use of the percentile rank is sufficient to provide the teacher and student with an idea of where he stands in relation to the national sample. Standard scores are usually computed so the average or mean score is 50 or 500. The scores are then distributed so that 34 percent of the scores fall between 40–50 (400–500), 34 percent between 50–60 (500–600), 14 percent between 30–40 (300–400), 14 percent between 60–70 (600–700), 2 percent between 20–30 (200–300), 2 percent between 70–80 (700–800). Thus, with standard scores the range is from 20 to 80 (200 to 800); the lowest 2 percent will receive standard scores between 20–30, the next higher 14 percent will receive standard scores between 30–40, and so forth.

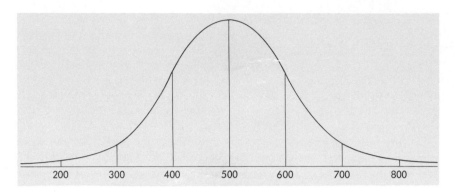

A comparison of this diagram with that for standard deviation on page 54 will show that each 10-point (100-point) band represents one standard deviation. Therefore, a score that is 1.2 standard deviations above the mean would be 62 (620) in standard score; a score .65 below the mean would be written 43.5 (435). This type of standard score is a straight linear transformation. At least one music test has standard scores of a slightly different sort called *normalized standard scores*. These alter any slight fluctuations in the normal curve achieved by a group of students to fit 68 percent of the group within one standard deviation of the mean, an additional 28 percent within two standard deviations, and the final 4 percent within the third standard deviation away from the mean. This is an area transformation, sometimes described as "forcing the scores into the normal curve." This procedure is most common when the standardization sample is small and somewhat unreliable.

Scores can also be reported as *z* scores. These relate to the standard deviation and take a form such as +1.2 or −.65, meaning 1.2 standard deviations above the mean, and .65 of one standard deviation below the mean. Norms may be in the form of *z* scores rather than raw scores, percentiles, or some other form. The uses of pluses and minuses is cumbersome when the score is to be combined with other scores; in addition, they may not be meaningful to the teacher until he has used the normal curve enough to become completely familiar with it.

The relative merits of each kind of standard score appear to be about equal. The greatest disadvantage in using *z* scores or the standard deviation is their tendency to overemphasize differences near the mean, where a change of one point in the score is relatively nondiscriminating, and to underemphasize the difference in scores at the extremes. In the center of the normal curve, where most of the students score, the difference between .1 and .2 (standard score 51 and 52 or 510 and 520) may not be as important as the difference in the third standard deviation between 2.1 and 2.2 (standard score 71 and 72 or 710 and 720). Because so many students achieve the same or similar scores, a difference of one question could change the position on the normal curve. At either extreme, the scores of students may vary considerably even among the top or bottom 5 percent, and one's relative position may not be affected by one or two questions.

OTHER DERIVED SCORES

There are many types of derived scores, all of them based upon some version of the normal curve. Two examples will illustrate the process used in obtaining a derived score. The *stanine* is one example. The normal curve is divided into nine scores according to this formula: the lowest stanine, 1, is two standard deviations below the mean; stanine 2 is 1.5 standard deviations below the mean; and so on, stanine 5 representing the mean, stanine 9, the highest, being two standard deviations above the mean. This system was widely used by the U.S. Air Force during World War II to provide a meaningful interpretation of raw scores. With the stanine the following percentages are used.

Score:	1	2	3	4	5	6	7	8	9	
Percentage of total population	4%	7%	12%	17%	20%	17%	12%	7%	4%	highest

The *sten* is another normalized standard score with five units on either side of the mean. General consensus seems to be that the standard score will eventually replace these derived scores. Three music tests use the standard score (see Chapter Eight).

STANDARD ERROR

Standard error of measurement, a numerical figure, indicates the possible distance that an individual's test score may deviate from his true score on the test. Thus, it is an indicator of the reliability of the test. It is usually referred to simply as standard error. Occasionally, standard deviation is called standard error of the mean or just standard error; the reader must look carefully to determine which definition is being used. Whereas standard deviation indicates the spread of scores for the entire population, standard error indicates the error factor for one individual on a particular test. Scores vary due to factors of attention, motivation, physical conditions, and environmental conditions, so that one person taking the same test several times would show some variation in his score for the test. His scores would follow the normal distribution pattern shown on page 52, only much smaller. This pattern of individual variance is called standard error.

For example, if a person were to be repeatedly tested using a test having a standard error of 3, we could expect his test score to be within 3 points on either side of his true score 68 percent of the times he takes the test, and within 6 points on either side of his true score 95 percent of the time. Thus, in interpreting test scores, each individual score is seen not as a point but as a range within which the individual's achievement on the test lies. The Gordon *Musical Aptitude Profile* provides a standard error of measurement of 8.6 for fifth-grade students in raw score units. This means that 68 percent of the time a fifth-grade student's true score would be within 8.6 points on either side of his actual raw score. Therefore, if his raw score is 46, the most accurate way to interpret his achievement on the test is to consider his true score as being between 37 and 55. Raw scores must be converted to standard scores for the Gordon test; if the standard score were 46, the standard error of measurement of the standard score would be 1.9, so the student's true score would be between 44 and 48 with 68 percent assurance; with 95 percent assurance it would be between 42 and 50. With single measurements a low standard error is desired because of the importance of the decision based on the test score. Most aptitude tests recommend that critical decisions not be based on aptitude test scores alone. Achievement tests and other evaluations should be used in conjunction with aptitude tests.

The standard error of measurement is affected by the number of questions on the test, the greater number of questions producing a larger standard error. The Farnum test has 40 questions with a standard error ranging from 2.3 to 3.4, whereas the Gordon test has 250 questions and a standard error ranging from 5.7 to 8.6. However, the two tests are comparable, for the parts of the Gordon test that contain 40 questions have measurement error of from 2.0 to 3.3 points. The larger standard error of measurement should not be interpreted negatively, for the longer test is the more reliable, other things being equal. Measurement is more exact with the longer test, as may be seen by the fact that the standard error, though bigger for the Gordon test, actually represents a smaller fraction of the standard deviation than does the standard error for the Farnum test. Thus, one can have more confidence in the percentiles given. Standard error is rarely considered in selecting a test or in choosing between two alternative tests, but it is of concern in reporting scores accurately.

Use of a *profile chart* in interpreting results has several advantages. A chart is maintained for each student, and every measurement score is placed on it so that evaluation of his progress can easily be made on the basis of all possible items. Where raw scores are used, comparisons between test scores are difficult; use of percentiles simplifies the process of finding the student's strengths and weaknesses as they are illustrated by the profile chart. An even better method is to use both percentile and raw score, so that all the information one might need is present on the chart.

Improving learning means emphasis upon individual test scores, individual learning problems, and individual goals. The concern in music should be to work with students as persons who differ in both achievement and potential, rather than to think of them as "band boys," "concert choir," or "this year's class." Even the tests given to provide curriculum data usually measure in terms of individuals: student A has greater strength here than student B, but B did better than A on another area, and so forth. In providing insights, rewards, motivation, or punishment, the immediacy of feedback, which is so important in learning, must be applied to individuals.

ITEM ANALYSIS

Among the procedures used in interpreting test results, one of the best is *item analysis*. Item analysis is also used in constructing tests, questionnaires and various types of checklists. As the term itself indicates, each test item is analyzed to find out how good a question it is, *goodness* referring to the difficulty of the question, the quality of the distractors where the question is multiple-choice, and to the ability of the question to discriminate between better and poorer students.

Only four of the standardized music tests in print today report item analysis. Item analysis for each question, by grade level, is helpful data for the teacher and should be included in any good test, although only one music test does so at present.

Item analysis consists of two parts: (1) determining the difficulty of the item and (2) determining its discrimination power. It is often computed by statistical formulas, but similar results may be obtained from a simple procedure. The first step is to place all of the papers in rank order, from top to bottom. A certain percentage of the best and the poorest is then selected, the normal recommendation being the top 27 percent and the bottom 27 percent. This percentage is not arbitrary; the top and bottom fourth or third will provide basically the same results. The assumption is made that the middle group of papers will follow the same general pattern as the two extremes. For each question on the test, a tabulation is made of the number of high achievers answering it correctly and the number of low achievers answering it correctly. These figures are then used with the following formula to find the discriminating power:

$$D = \frac{\text{Uppers - lowers}}{\text{the number in one group}}$$
or ½ the total number.

For example, if the class had a total of fifty-five students, 27 percent of these would be 15, so the fifteen top papers and the fifteen lowest papers would be examined. In the upper 27 percent, eleven answered Question one correctly; in the lower 27 percent, eight students answered Question one correctly. The formula is

$$D = \frac{11 - 8}{15} = \frac{3}{15} = .20.$$

The discrimination index for Question 1, then, is .20 and is positive, indicating that more good students answered the question correctly than poor students. Discrimination can range from -1.00 to a $+1.00$. Usually, the larger the positive value of the number the better, although other qualities of the test item are more important than the size of the discrimination index.

The relative difficulty of the question is computed by the formula

$$\text{Difficulty} = \frac{\text{No. right}}{\text{No. students.}}$$

With 30 students in a class, 19 answering correctly, the problem would be

$$\text{Difficulty} = \frac{19}{30} = .63.$$

Difficulty can range from .00 where there are no correct answers to 1.00 where the entire group answers the question correctly. Computing difficulty is somewhat more accurate when the entire class is used rather than only the upper and lower extremes.

The information supplied by item analysis is helpful when applied with common sense. Discriminating power is related to difficulty, because a question obviously cannot discriminate when it is so easy that everyone answers it correctly. However, in the center range of difficulty the relationship between it and discrimination is not direct. For example, in working with a sample of sixteen high test papers and sixteen low papers, half of each group might answer Question 2 correctly, in which case the difficulty index would be .50 and the discrimination index would be .00. If all the high papers but none of the low papers answered Question 2 correctly, the difficulty index would again be .50, but the discrimination index 1.00. As may be seen from the example, at the .50 index of difficulty, the highest discrimination is possible; as the difficulty index rises above .50, a larger percentage of students will obtain correct answers and the possible discrimination level lowers. However, to have all of the test items at .50 difficulty would not necessarily make a better test. A guideline is that there should be no question that everyone answers correctly and no question that everyone misses; all those taking the test should be able to correctly answer some of the items, but no one should be able to make a perfect score. Test makers often strive for a range of difficulty from .20 to .80, with most of the items from .40 to .70. Questions above or below this range are usually dropped and not included in the final version of a published test.

The difficulty index can be used with achievement tests to discover whether the test material is actually the content of the music program. If the questions are easier for students in the higher grades and more difficult for those in the lower grades, this may indicate that some of the test content is being taught in the school music program. Tests that are too easy must be avoided because they do not give the teacher any information at all. The easy test penalizes the good student by not giving him a chance to show what he can do better than the average or below-average student. In an aptitude test, little decrease in difficulty would be expected for older students, since aptitude, by definition, remains constant.

In achievement tests, item difficulty can contribute to the improvement of instruction and to motivation. The review of a test is often as valuable as preparing for it and taking it. Where the questions are easy enough that the majority of the class answers them correctly, the need for a review of the test is small. Items of sufficient difficulty to help locate misconceptions or lack of comprehension are useful means to better learning. Errors can be corrected, generalities can be interpreted and applied, and facts can be reinforced in the test review.

Item discrimination may be misleading and requires careful scrutiny of the questions themselves. In a multiple-choice question that most of the students are missing, the alternative answers should be inspected and discrimination indices computed for them. If students are all choosing the same wrong answer, the information involved may have been poorly taught or taught incorrectly with resulting misconceptions. Where a four-choice answer is offered, the ideal question will have three incorrect answers that all attract some response, preferably from the lower half of the class. Where students tend to rule out two of the four choices and choose primarily between the correct answer and one foil, the question is no longer true multiple-choice but has become a true-false question for all practical purposes.

Other information from item discrimination may suggest problems. If the better students miss a question and the poorer ones answer it correctly, is it a poor question? The answer is usually yes. Poor students may be getting it correct because they have memorized a term or a fact that seems to fit with something in the question, while the better students are misled because of poor wording or an incomplete idea that they interpret erroneously as a clue. Such a question should be deleted, replaced with a better one, or at least ignored in the scoring. Another question often raised about discrimination is whether test items with low discrimination are good. Again, the item itself must be scrutinized. A question may be valid but have low discrimination because the information has not been taught; neither the good students nor the poor ones know the right answer. The question is valid if the concept is one that should be included in learning. Because one of the purposes of achievement tests is to improve instruction, numerous items may have low discrimination but high validity and be entirely appropriate for the test; instruction will improve when tests set high standards. Once the teacher teaches these facts and understandings, the discrimination index for such items will rise.

Because item analysis is related to the total test, questions requiring a different type of skill from that used for most of the test may have low discrimination. In other words, the students who can do well on most of the test items will make high scores. However, a section calling for different skills may result in several incorrect answers from the high scoring students, and those test items will appear to have low discrimination because they do not separate high scorers from low scorers.

If the test is being used primarily as a measurement of achievement upon which to base grades or make selections, then item discrimination is much more important than where the test is a learning device, to evaluate the effectiveness of the program, or to improve instruction. The higher the item discrimination, the more fair the measurement. With the previous exceptions, item discrimination should be above .20. Aptitude tests are usually easier than achievement tests and, therefore, have high difficulty indices, around .60 or .70. Items on an achievement test of .60 or .70 that are good test items with respect to validity and reliability may have very high discrimination because a correct answer will be a good indication that the item has been taught and learned. The present status of learning in the music program of many public schools is such that high indices cannot be expected, for students have not been exposed to the most elementary terms and concepts.

In using item analysis for classroom tests, computations for both difficulty and discrimination must be accepted as tentative because the number of students involved is insufficient to establish reliability.

Adding or subtracting three or four student scores could influence the indices noticeably. The computations for large samples on standardized tests are more reliable. This is not to discourage the teacher from a close analysis of his own test, but is a warning that the analysis must be accepted with care.

DISSEMINATION

One of the easier subjects to discuss is the manner in which scores may be reported to students or other interested persons. The first point to make is that scores of some sort should always be reported to the student who has taken the test. A standardized test covering a wide area of learning is sometimes given because the teacher feels he should. If the results are discouraging to the teacher or if he does not have the knowledge to understand the implications of the scores, he may decide not to disseminate them to students. He may mistrust the whole testing situation anyway and feel that his duty is done when the scores are recorded. So the scores are filed away in a safe place and promptly forgotten. Such a procedure is a wasteful expenditure of school monies and class time, and may also undermine student morale. A test is important to a student, and he wants to know how he did on it. The student may be given his raw score; he can then compare his score with his peers as he does for most classroom tests. Basically, however, the raw score is of little use. Percentiles have more meaning and are specific enough to satisfy the student. Of more accuracy is a percentile band, which shows the range in which the student's score lies, for it accounts for possible errors in the score.

Anastasi[3] states that test scores are to be released only to persons qualified to interpret them. This is too narrow an interpretation of evaluation, for it is concerned with learning as an abstract phenomenon rather than with the instruction of students. Students want to know test scores and are frustrated or discouraged when this information is withheld. Gronlund[4] cites a study by Page illustrating the value of reporting test results to students. Test papers for students in grades 7 through 12 were scored and then sorted into three piles at random. For the first pile, specific comments were written in addition to the grade, on the second pile general comments plus the grade, and for the third pile only the grade was written with no comment. Further improvement was in rela-

---

[3] Anne Anastasi, *Psychological Testing*, 3rd ed. (New York: The Macmillan Company, 1968), p. 31.

[4] Norman Gronlund, *Measurement and Evaluation in Teaching* (New York: The Macmillan Company, 1965), p. 365.

tion to the comments made, those students with no comments on their test papers making the least improvement. For students as well as for adults, working toward a remote goal has little meaning; for example, to work towards an appreciation of great music is like working toward an understanding of biology. Unless there are many instructional goals to be aimed at and tested for, and unless the achievement is examined, faraway abstract goals hold no motivating power.

QUESTIONS FOR DISCUSSION

1. In choir this year, all the sopranos obtained the correct answer to a question with a difficulty index of .78 and a discrimination index of .45. On another question all the tenors obtained the correct answer with a difficulty index of .42, discrimination of .45. What interpretation could you make?

2. This year, you had five students in your class of twenty-five score more than two standard deviations above the mean on *Music Achievement Test* 2. How would you interpret this to their parents?

3. You wish to interpret test scores as fairly as possible to a student. He scored at the 45th percentile on a test with a standard deviation of 12.3, mean of 58, standard error of 1.2. His raw score is 52. Percentile score for 64 is 67th percentile, 53 is 47th percentile, 77 is 82nd percentile, 54 is 48th percentile, 51 is 43rd percentile, 50 is 42nd percentile, 40 is 35th percentile, 27 is 22nd percentile. What will you tell him?

4. What measures of central tendency seem to be most appropriate for interpreting:
   (a) aptitude scores of all fifth-grade students?
   (b) achievement scores of students studying private piano?
   (c) music contest ratings?

REFERENCES

Ahmann, J. Stanley, and Marvin Glock, *Evaluating Pupil Growth* (2nd ed.). Boston: Allyn and Bacon, Inc., 1963, Chapter 6.

Gronlund, Norman, *Measurement and Evaluation in Teaching.* New York: The Macmillan Company, 1965, Chapter 14 and Part V.

Lyman, Howard, *Test Scores and What They Mean.* Englewood Cliffs, N.J.: Prentice-Hall, Inc., 1963, Chapters 5, 11.

Mehrens, William A., and Irvin Lehmann, *Standardized Tests in Education*. New York: Holt, Rinehart & Winston, Inc., 1969, Chapter 1.

Stanley, Julian, *Measurement in Today's Schools* (4th ed.). Englewood Cliffs, N.J.: Prentice-Hall, Inc., 1964, Chapter 3.

Wood, Dorothy Adkins, *Test Construction: Development and Interpretation of Achievement Tests*. Columbus, Ohio: Charles E. Merrill Books, Inc., 1961, Chapter 8.

CHAPTER FOUR

evaluating musical aptitude

The identification of musical talent has caught the imagination of musicians and psychologists to an extent unique in psychological research. Relatively little interest has been displayed in the psychological factors of music teaching and learning per se, but much effort has been expended upon defining musical talent, identifying its components, and creating tools that could measure these traits. This unusual interest, over the past six or seven decades, has undoubtedly affected the music profession in several ways. Those musicians who scoff at the objective approaches of psychology have also been inclined to reject any intrusion of psychology into the field of music, perhaps because the identification of musical aptitude has not convinced many, despite all of its flurry and furor. Leadership that could have been invested in the consideration of how children learn and how they should be taught has been expended in the attempt to pin down the elusive qualities of talent. Further, commercial interests have taken advantage of this obvious concern and have published their own *measures* of talent, whose sole aim is to aid the sale of instruments.

Why the identification of musical aptitude should hold such fascination is not clear. Perhaps the answer lies in the value men have traditionally placed upon musical talent. Through the centuries, the secular princes as well as the princes of the church surrounded themselves with the best talent—even, as with Haydn, stooping to thievery to secure it. In the golden age of Italian opera, identification of youthful talent was necessary to obtain the spectacular *castrati,* who dazzled public and private audiences alike. In recent times, municipal and state subsidies have in Europe replaced the former patronage of the nobility, and even in the United States instances may be found of city, state, and federal support for music and other arts. These, together with the paying public, attest to the monetary value we place on talent.

DEFINING MUSICAL APTITUDE

At the present time, we have not yet been able to state positively what constitutes musical talent or aptitude. It may be somewhat akin to intelligence, and we may be able to develop measures with which we can obtain a rating of musical intelligence. Those who work with I.Q. tests are careful to delimit their results: intelligence is defined as ability to deal successfully with certain mental tasks, such as problem solving or the acquisition of facts and concepts. There are many areas of human behavior and of learning that intelligence does not encompass. Recent research indicates that musicality is at least as complex as intelligence.

If an individual has the ability to listen to art music with pleasure and understanding, but has no performance skill, is he musical? Is the performer musical who performs with skill and with a depth of musical feeling, but depends upon a teacher to lead him? Is the composer who works in avant-garde media and has little interest in or patience for the music of the past musical? What about the singer or instrumentalist whose sight-reading is full of glaring errors in pitch, rhythm, and tempo, but who can with much repetition reach an exciting state of performance? As Lars Holmstrom states, "Nevertheless, it may be maintained without much fear of contradiction that even today the concept of musicality has no uniform and functional purport."[1] The range of musical skills and competencies extends from cymbal playing to composing and scoring a large work for 100 instruments. All of the examples can be musical, though there is little doubt that some require greater skill than others. Does the greater skill imply greater musicianship? In addition to the problem of definition the question of learned versus inherent musicality has been the focus of numerous studies.

---

[1] Lars Gunnar Holmstrom, *Musicality and Prognosis,* Studia Scientiae Paedagogical Upsaliensia V (Norstedts: Svenska-Bokförlaget, 1963), p. 13.

There appear to be several kinds of musical talent or several facets to it, such as talent for performance, for composition, for musicological research, for conducting, and perhaps for listening. Therefore, one purpose of musical aptitude tests should be to determine the minimum below which success in any of these fields would not be possible. Perhaps another, lower minimum would be established to determine those who could profit from musical training. If the answer to this latter problem were that all persons could profit, much of the usefulness of aptitude tests would be automatically eliminated, and their development could be geared toward locating individuals with professional potential. Many musical aptitude tests have been designed as measures to discover talent for performance potential and not to determine general musicality. Validation has usually been accomplished through correlation with performance skills rather than with skills needed for musical criticism, creativity, or other facets mentioned above. The real value of testing is not the ability to predict but rather the ability to improve learning by giving direction to the learning efforts of students and teachers.

APTITUDE VERSUS ACHIEVEMENT

The problem of separating aptitude from achievement is a tough one, for some aspects of musical development seemingly cannot be measured until the child is relatively mature, and by this time much learning, or achievement, has occurred. Whether musical talent is inherited or learned, it appears in varying qualities early in life before much formal learning has taken place. Measurement has traditionally come later and has focused on certain abilities, which seem to be affected very little by drill or by exercises designed to improve them; these abilities may represent aptitude, since they are present in varying quantities. Therefore, one definition for music aptitude is that it consists of those qualities that are developed over a long period of time. Achievement consists of those qualities that are measurable within short periods—a week, a month, a school year. Sensitivity to pitch and intonation differences would be a quality of aptitude: although small children can early differentiate between high and low (when they know the musical definition of these terms), ability to hear minute differences in intonation is considered to be aptitude because it develops over a long period of time and in many cases ceases to improve despite further training. Tonal memory is also considered to be aptitude, for it improves slowly and is possessed in widely varying quantities that seem not to be directly related to length of experience. College freshman theory courses contain both students who can write down a simple four-measure melody after one or two hearings and other students who may be unable to match this feat after two semesters of practice and instruction. Some aptitude measures use preference tests and other tasks that seem to be readily influenced by training. The identification of sufficient tasks that are characteristic of musical people, whether inherited or learned slowly, is at the heart of determining the validity and usefulness of these tests. Lehman feels that an exact definition of aptitude is not a necessary requisite to good tests. He states that intelligence could be measured before it could be defined and that the same may be true of music aptitude.[2]

There are indications that ability to differentiate between major and minor, to recognize the tonal center, to read music, to determine the basic pulse, and so on, may be learned at any period of one's life and within a relatively short time. Music-reading skill is improved with practice, it will deteriorate when not used, and it can be developed to a fantastically complicated level such as that possessed by composers and conductors whose eyes and mind can follow a dozen instrumental parts and obtain an accurate impression of a new composition without hearing it. Until more is known about music aptitude, this differentiation between it and achievement is probably the most reasonable and workable one. When the teacher recognizes the distinction between these two general qualities and can determine which musical acts pertain to aptitude and which to achievement, he can be more realistic about student attainment and more demanding of progress in those skills that can be improved readily. So far, music teachers have neither given much thought to what they expect from aptitude tests nor used the tests imaginatively. Knowledge of ability can aid in sectioning, can permit individualized and special teaching techniques, and can increase motivation. Knowledge of talent potential is critical for forming expectations, a necessary part of teaching.

For the purpose of student selection, most subject matter fields depend upon interest and preference tests with primary emphasis upon records of past achievement. Tests of learning ability (i.e. aptitude) that seem to be the most accurate predictors of academic success are those that look like general achievement tests for a more elementary level of learning. Because all test scores measure some type of educational potential, distinguishing between a score on a talent test and one on an achievement test in the same subject is almost impossible. We find little use of aptitude tests at the college entrance level, for the student's high school record is a better predictor than any single test, whether aptitude or

2 Paul Lehman, *Tests and Measurements in Music* (Englewood Cliffs, N.J.: Prentice-Hall, Inc., 1968), p. 8.

achievement. If good music programs existed for students at the levels where music is required—usually grades 1 through 6—and if teachers were systematic in observing and recording the process of their students in the important aspects of musical development, then selection of students for further training would present no problem. The record of achievement would clearly show the potential. Aptitude tests could then assume the role of guiding the selection of appropriate learning experiences for gifted students and the formulation of long-range plans for all students.

APTITUDE TESTS

Several measures of musical aptitude are presently in use. In England, the Wing Musical Intelligence Test and the Bentley *Measures of Musical Abilities* have general acceptance; the Seashore *Measures of Musical Talent* and the Gordon *Musical Aptitude Profile* are well known in the United States. Considerable experimental work has been done in the Scandinavian countries with Franklin's[3] and Holmstrom's[4] measures; these are not available in published form in the United States. Still in print and presumably still in use are the Kwalwasser *Music Talent Test,* the Kwalwasser-Dykema *K-D Music Tests,* the Tilson-Gretsch Test for Musical Aptitude, and the *Drake Musical Aptitude Tests.* All of these except Franklin and Holmstrom are described in detail in Chapter Eight.

If music teachers desire to make talent evaluations for specialized musical activities, they must make careful identification of these activities in behavioral terms so that the appropriate test or tool may be employed. The music teacher must realize that the authors of good aptitude tests usually do not make extensive claims for their products; misrepresentation comes from word-of-mouth advertising, from misinterpretation of the written statements about the tests, or from other musicians who are only partially informed. For instance, Seashore states in the 1939 manual that his tests represent merely one specific capacity or talent; that numerous other capacities are also required for success in music; that wherever possible these measures should be employed in connection with case histories and auditions; and that no one should make recommendations without becoming familiar with some of the studies on auditory ability and musical achievement that he lists in the bibliography of the test manual. His main point is that more than one measure of aptitude is necessary, and he himself makes no provision for a composite grade for the total set of

---

[3] Erik Franklin, *Tonality as a Basis for Musical Talent* (Göteborg: Gumperts Förlag, 1956).

[4] Holmstrom, *Musicality and Prognosis.*

tests, but instead encourages inspection of the several scores in determining talent.

Readiness tests provide the teacher with similar information. The instrumental teacher is concerned about readiness in terms of eye-hand coordination, music reading, physical development, and perhaps other factors in addition to talent potential. A preinstrument program can provide readiness information based on work with rhythm instruments, recorders, or similar musical instruments if the program emphasizes music-reading activities and has some form of systematic evaluation. The general music teacher is concerned about readiness for music reading, for formal training in rhythmic development, and for specific listening experiences. Although a preprogram is one way of determining readiness, there are more efficient ways than involving all the children in a six-week (or longer) instructional program. Tests can provide much of the same information. Ability to distinguish pitch, to repeat rhythms, or to follow a simple line score in listening to a short work are some tasks that provide excellent clues to readiness and are often used in instrumental music. The readiness stages and indicators of Piaget might be useful in general music. Wing and Bentley have indicated a readiness age of 10 or 11 for hearing the number of voices in a chord. For preschool or kindergarten instrumental instruction, such as is given in strings and piano, some parent interest and attitude is a necessary part of the readiness for the child's success at this age depends upon his parent's devotion to the goal. Readiness indicators change. At the fourth-grade level, readiness for instrumental instruction might include ability to repeat a sung melody, ability to match pitch, rhythmic perception, and physical characteristics. At the seventh-grade level, such readiness would probably also include ability to read music or at least follow the notation. Readiness for college-level music, whether performance, theory, or history, is almost always based upon past achievement, although a battery of tests that included a valid aptitude test coupled with achievement tests and records would provide the best information for planning purposes.

APTITUDE FOR MUSIC TEACHING

In the area of teacher preparation, other measures besides aptitude and achievement are necessary to predict success with student teaching. Musicians like to believe that the more musical one is, the more successful he will be as a teacher; all evidence indicates this is not so. Some of the best teachers of music are elementary classroom teachers who know more about pedagogy than about any one subject matter area. Minimums are necessary for every area of knowledge to be taught, even at the first-grade level, and knowledge above the minimum certainly adds to the potentiality for successful teaching. Beyond that, however, are factors such as interest in and commitment to teaching, personality and leadership abilities, knowledge of methods and materials. These apply to all areas of teaching including music. Musicality is often judged on the basis of performing ability in one's major area, undoubtedly an inefficient and inaccurate way to form the judgment. Technique, diligence, and the careful guidance of a good teacher may combine to give the student performer the appearance of greater musicality than is really the case. What constitutes minimums of musicianship, personality, and other factors requisite for the finished product of a good prospective teacher must be determined by norms, either national or local. Those schools that believe psychological measures are important in evaluating student potential should establish local norms for the tests in this area.

The amount of time and expense invested in making a decision is dependent upon how important the decision is. When a new drug is being tested that cures most of the time but occasionally kills, what percentage of error is acceptable? For the research laboratory, one error in 100 would probably not be acceptable, but with educational research, the 1 percent error is considered highly acceptable. No one ever really dies from new educational methods. When a new curriculum is being tested against the old, if the new appears to be better in ninety-nine instances out of one hundred, it would most assuredly be adopted. Similarly, guiding a student into instrumental study is not a major decision; if the prognosis is wrong, the ill effects are to be found only in some wasted time and money. On the other hand, decisions as to whether a student should be allowed to enter college as a music major, or to student teach, or to be graduated from a school of music are important for the student and the institution as well as for the future students of this potential teacher. The evidence gathered to help make such decisions should be many-faceted, as accurate as possible, and must be meaningful in terms that compare this student with graduates and nongraduates of the university. Often, it appears that more effort is given to objectivity in measuring third-grade talent than in determining fitness for teaching.

Proper interpretation of aptitude and achievement test scores is necessary when making important decisions. In a comparison of a high school senior's music achievement scores with that of other high school seniors, the prospective music major should score above the 90th percentile and perhaps above the 95th. However, if the comparison is with entering college freshman music majors, a score at the 50th percentile or lower would be acceptable. A rating on performance should be compared with college freshman music majors or, for a more stringent comparison, with freshman piano majors, these scores usually being the highest. If these two scores appear satisfactorily high and if the student's aptitude scores are well above average, his decision to major in music would seem to be a sound one. If aptitude scores contradict the achievement and performance scores, the best approach is to administer the aptitude test again. If several years have passed since the earlier scores were derived, some gain might be expected, though rarely a significant one.

PROMOTION TALENT TESTS

It is a sad commentary on the music profession that promotion talent tests furnished by instrument manufacturers enjoy wider use than seriously constructed measures. The chance scores and the spurious norms on these tests can easily be noted. These exercises, for they are really not tests, can serve little purpose in any honest attempt at guidance. However, the blame for such exercises does not lie entirely with the manufacturing companies. Company officials realize that the grading systems used for music are not valid, and so little music is taught that records of past achievement will not discriminate any more than will check marks of satisfactory progress in general music. Teachers seem to want some tool upon which to depend in guiding students into instrumental music, and since they have been unwilling to use the legitimately constructed measures, instrumental companies have filled the need by supplying their own tests. Promotion talent tests provide a good example of the importance of evaluation, however, for in spite of the lack of scholarship in their construction, one still knows more by using them than by not using them.

Talent evaluation and guidance have often included an appraisal of motor skill and physical characteristics. Concern has been displayed for digital dexterity, length of arms for trombone and violin players, independence of hands for percussionists, size of hands for pianists, thickness of lips for wind instrumentalists, and various other nonmusical attributes. In vocational and technical education, tests are used for manual dexterity, and these may be appropriate. The few research studies that have used such tests for potential music ability have found them not to discriminate. At present, only extreme cases of physical abnormality seem to be important as factors in instrumental aptitude.

QUESTIONS FOR DISCUSSION

1. What areas have been identified by test makers as possibly measuring music talent? Do these agree with the characteristics you and others look for in identifying "musical" people?

2. Describe different types of talent needed by the performer, the composer, the musicologist, etc. What talents do they share?

3. At what age level is "musicality" first apparent in child prodigies and how is it usually identified?

4. Assuming the preference sections of the *Wing Musical Intelligence Test* and the *Musical Aptitude Profile* are valid, what implications does this have for music programs, objectives, and methods?

5. What abilities measured by other aptitude tests appear to be inherited, learned primarily before school age, or learned over a long period of time?

REFERENCES

Lundin, Robert, *An Objective Psychology of Music* (2nd ed.). New York: The Ronald Press Company, 1967.

Révész, G., *Introduction to the Psychology of Music*. Norman, Okla.: University of Oklahoma Press, 1954.

Seashore, Carl, *The Psychology of Musical Talent*. Morristown, N.J.: Silver Burdett Company, 1919.

Shuter, Rosamund, *The Psychology of Musical Ability*. London: Methuen & Co. Ltd., 1968, Part III.

Stodola, Quentin, and Kalmer Stordahl, *Basic Educational Tests and Measurement*. Chicago: Science Research Associates, Inc., 1967, Chapter 5.

Whybrew, William, *Measurement and Evaluation in Music*. Dubuque, Iowa: Wm. C. Brown Company, Publishers, 1962, Chapters 6, 8.

CHAPTER FIVE

evaluating cognitive learning

THE PLACE OF COGNITIVE LEARNING

The cognitive aspects of music learning are perhaps the easiest to teach, to discuss, and to evaluate. They are the easiest to define in behavorial terms and to evaluate against the objectives. Teaching for cognitive learning is appropriate at every age and at every stage of development, from preschool experiences through postdoctoral study, for it is the nature of facts that they can be extremely simple or vastly complicated. Learning the name of an item is learning a fact; so is the working out of a set of interrelationships. The child begins by learning what a *song* is, a *melody,* or a *drum.* When he arrives at the level of university music major a large part of his education will be in the cognitive domain, in music theory and history, psychology, professional education, and music literature. Much instructional effort in music has rightly been devoted to knowledge about music, but so often to the point where the other aspects of musical learning have been neglected. Having knowledge about music, however, does not appear to be harmful to the fullest understanding and appreciation; on the contrary, it seems to enhance it. Further, there is no evidence that the amount of knowledge presently taught in the public schools excludes giving attention to the affective aspects and the skill aspects of music. With the increase in programed learning, computer-assisted instruction, and other sophisticated teaching aids, the objectives for cognitive learning in music should be more easily achieved, and even surpassed, without slighting other phases of musical endeavor.

There is hardly an area of living in which cognition is not important, and though we are prone to emphasize the subjective and emotional nature of music, knowledge is essential to valid experiences with music. Only with knowledge can the emotional response be transformed into the truly aesthetic response, the performer's skills create honest and appropriate interpretations of the composer's intent, the passing musical interest of the public school student be retained as a lifelong pursuit for recreation. The elementary and secondary schools often devote too little time to cognitive learning while at the same time basing evaluation of progress upon cognitive measurement. Indeed, the role of factual learning has become so small in the public school music curricula that a musical vocabulary is almost totally absent at all ages, and courses such as music history and theory are unique, seemingly beyond the interest of the ordinary music student and requiring some kind of specialized skill or previous training.

The negative connotation placed upon cognitive learning in music stems from the 1920s and 1930s, when instruction emphasized identification of notes, syllables, key signatures, and titles of compositions, and failed to apply these to musical experiences or to find meaningful ways to teach them. Rather than recognizing that the problem lay in the method of teaching rather than in the content itself, teachers quickly dropped content and placed emphasis upon activities.

Good teaching must utilize and foster the development of all three areas of learning: psychomotor, cognitive, and affective. Furthermore, combining all three areas in musical experiences is probably the most sound approach to teaching the majority of the time, though many instances will arise when one domain will need to be isolated and emphasized. Evaluating is approached differently from teaching, and here the three areas of learning should usually be separated for diagnostic purposes to ensure accurate judgments. Thus, the following pages offer numerous suggestions for ways in which cognitive learning may be measured alone.

TEACHER-CONSTRUCTED TESTS

Teacher-constructed tests are a necessity for evaluation in the cognitive area. Even if new standardized tests become available for this important area, these cannot completely replace teacher-constructed tests directed at the specific program of the local situation. Teachers, therefore, need to know as much as possible about test construction in order to produce good tools for use in daily teaching. Questions dealing with facts can have numerous pitfalls: they may be too easy, so that they have no discriminating power; they may be worded so that the correct answer is implied or so that the reader is misled; a bad question may confuse the good student who recognizes an error in the wording, while it elicits the correct answer from the more superficial reader; the question may be one in which guessing is facilitated. For these reasons, if a test is being constructed for repeated or important use, making an item analysis can show which questions discriminate and have the proper difficulty for the group and which questions should be improved or dropped.

Included in the kinds of written questions that may be created to test factual learning are the following: true-false, multiple-choice with a single correct answer, multiple-choice with two or more correct answers or an indefinite number of correct answers, matching questions one-to-one, matching questions in which a single item may answer more than one question, finding the error(s) in a sentence, finding the error(s) in the musical score, sentence completion (one word), sentence completion (short-answer), identification (short or lengthy answer), reading a paragraph and answering questions, reading a short musical excerpt and answering questions. Other activities besides written questions and written answers can be used to evaluate cognition. *Spell downs* putting members of the class against each other, oral questions, and informal discussions in class or in rehearsals can serve for occasional general indications of learning. Tasks such as transposing a musical excerpt to another key, in writing rather than by playing, have some value for measuring one kind of cognition. A similar task might be to insert meter signature and bar lines in a simple score or to translate the score into rhythmic values half the length or twice the length, etc. Depending upon the teacher's sophistication in measurement and the degree of complexity of the learning to be tested, many objective test items can be created besides the overworked and greatly loathed true-false question.

A TAXONOMY OF COGNITIVE OBJECTIVES

In any text on evaluation, the taxonomy of educational objectives must be discussed because one of the basic purposes of a taxonomy of objectives is to facilitate evaluation. The term *taxonomy* has been widely used to mean the classification of plants and animals, showing their natural botanical or biological relationships. In recent years it has also been applied to educational objectives, with the similar meaning of classification or organization that shows natural relationships. First worked out by a group of college examiners, one taxonomy is limited to educational goals in the cognitive area, by which is meant "activities such as remembering and recalling knowledge, thinking, problem solving, creating."[1] The value of the taxonomy is that it helps teachers and curriculum planners to examine goals, to think critically about the exact meaning of goals, and to classify them in a hierarchy that shows which goals are of a fundamental nature and which goals exist dependent upon those fundamental ones.

Bloom's taxonomy of cognitive objectives may seem cumbersome and irrelevant to the music teacher, who will be able to see little use for the tight, neat categories into which the various aspects of cognition have been placed. Bloom and his coauthors believe that the taxonomy does progress from simple to complex, so that an examination of the order in which the categories of learning have been placed *can* be very helpful for planning learning experiences. Its use in this chapter is to provide a guide for sample questions that the teacher may examine as he constructs tests for factual learning in the classroom. The sample questions, therefore, have two purposes: first, to help the reader understand what is implied by each category in the taxonomy, and second, to help illustrate the variety of ways in which objective questions may be presented. The taxonomy of educational objectives, cognitive domain, follows.[2]

1.00   Knowledge
   1.10   knowledge of specifics
   1.11   knowledge of terminology
   1.12   knowledge of specific facts
   1.20   knowledge of ways and means of dealing with specifics
   1.21   knowledge of conventions
   1.22   knowledge of trends and sequences
   1.23   knowledge of classifications and categories
   1.24   knowledge of criteria
   1.25   knowledge of methodology
   1.30   knowledge of the universals and abstractions in a field
   1.31   knowledge of principles and generalizations
   1.32   knowledge of theories and structures

2.00   Comprehension
   2.10   translation
   2.20   interpretation
   2.30   extrapolation

3.00   Application

4.00   Analysis

---

[1] Benjamin Bloom, ed., *Taxonomy of Educational Objectives: The Classification of Educational Goals, Handbook I: Cognitive Domain* (New York: David McKay Co., Inc., 1956), p. 2.

[2] *Ibid.,* pp. 201–207.

4.10   analysis of elements
4.20   analysis of relationships
4.30   analysis of organizational principles

5.00   Synthesis
    5.10   production of a unique communication
    5.20   production of a plan or proposed set of operations
    5.30   derivation of a set of abstract relations

6.00   Evaluation
    6.10   judgments in terms of internal evidence
    6.20   judgments in terms of external criteria

An inspection of the taxonomy reveals that it runs from concrete to abstract, from simple to complex. Even within the area of knowledge alone, the types of cognition become complex as one progresses toward the end. The public school teacher will be concerned primarily with knowledge—that is, remembering—though comprehension, application, and analysis surely have a place in musical learning.

1.00   KNOWLEDGE

Determining whether the student has a knowledge of terminology or conventions or abstractions in a field must be done largely through tests, for informal discussion or practical application can be an inaccurate mode for evaluating such knowledge. Some of the possible formats for test questions are presented below.

1.10 Knowledge of specifics. Specifics are of two types, either terminology or specific facts. A specific is an isolated bit of information, meaningful in itself.

1.11 Knowledge of terminology. For young children, oral response to flash cards, pictures, or the objects themselves can help measure knowledge of terminology. For children with some reading ability, matching the picture of the object with its name is feasible. For junior high level and above, the following questions would be appropriate for measuring knowledge of terminology.

[3] 1. A symphony can best be described as:

    (a) a number of movements, each in the character of a dance and all in the same key.
    (b) a type of nineteenth-century music based upon an extramusical idea, either poetic or descriptive.
    (c) a sonata for orchestra.
    (d) a composition for solo player and orchestra teamed on an equal basis.

---

[3] Questions used are examplars of the types that can be used. All possible types of probing information are not shown.

2. Match the definition in the second column with the musical term in the first column.

1. crescendo	a. gradually slackening in speed
2. accelerando	b. with motion
3. forte	c. increasing tone volume
4. allegro	d. pause
5. ritard	e. dying away
6. fermata	f. kindly, sympathetic
7. con moto	g. quick tempo
	h. loud
	i. becoming faster

1.12 Knowledge of specific facts. A fact may be simple or complex, but it offers more information than simply the name of something, as in terminology. A large body of facts exists that should be mastered by those who are *learning* music (rather than *taking* music). The following examples represent several different learning levels.

1. The Doctrine of Affections
   (a) was formulated by J. Quantz and C. P. E. Bach in the late eighteenth century and describes the aesthetic theory of the sensitive style.
   (b) was formulated by composers in the seventeenth century and describes an expressive vocal passage sung to one syllable.
   (c) describes the affected qualities of program music that developed in the nineteenth century.
   (d) describes the ornamented type of music that arose during the Baroque period.

2. About what proportion of the student body of high schools elects some form of music participation?
   (a) 10%   (b) 20%   (c) 35%   (d) 50%   (e) 60%

3. The usual number of bassoons in a symphony orchestra is:
   (a) more than   (b) less than   (c) the same as   the usual number of oboes in a symphony orchestra.

4. Arrange in chronological order:
   (a) Bach's B Minor Mass
   (b) Palestrina's *Missa Papae Marcelli*
   (c) Brahms' *A German Requiem*
   (d) Mozart's Requiem

1.20 Knowledge of ways and means of dealing with specifics. Various ways of dealing with specifics are given in the categories below. To know how to use a fact or how to relate it to other facts and terms is an advance in understanding beyond simple factual knowledge. Often, a fact is learned in relationship to other facts, but it may be learned in isolation. For a student to make use of the facts he learns, he must be taught the various ways and means of dealing with them.

1.21 Knowledge of conventions.   In musical learning, this category would include the compositional styles from various art periods; the conventions pertaining to various compositional forms; performance practices typical of various art periods and various compositional forms; stylistic characteristics of specific composers; the rules of harmony, theory, and counterpoint; translations of musical terms and signs that were interpreted differently in different art periods; and so forth.

1. The first movement of a sonata is commonly distinguished from the other movements by its greater
   (a) rapidity and gaiety.
   (b) length and complexity.
   (c) emotional abandon.
   (d) sweetness and charm.
   (e) structural informality.[4]

2. Blacken the appropriate answer space for each item according to the following:
   A if the statement applies to the symphonic poem.
   B if the statement applies to the fugue.
   C if the statement applies to the motet.
   D if the statement applies to the suite.
   E if the statement applies to the sonata.

   A   B   C   D   E
   || || || || || Mozart's Symphony in G minor, #40, though composed for orchestra, is representative of this type in the order and form of its movements.

   || || || || || This type of composition is based upon a "subject" and utilizes the principle of imitation.

   || || || || || Instrumental works representative of this type are usually based upon extra-musical ideas, either poetic or descriptive.

   || || || || || A work of this type may include among its different movements an overture or prelude, an air, and a gigue.

3. Draw a line through the wrong word or term in the following sentences, and write the correct word in the blank at the end of the sentence.
   (a) Castanets, tambourines, and clarinets are typical instruments used in gypsy music. _____
   (b) Marches are often written for string quartet or for band. _____

---

[4] *Ibid.,* p. 52.

(c) When a note is written with a dot beside it, we separate it somewhat from the following note. _____

1.22 Knowledge of trends and sequences. One of the broad objectives of public school music is that the student understand the ongoing process of musical expression, how developments arise, grow, culminate, and are transformed into further developments, and of the place each composer occupies in this ongoing process. Such understanding may be simple or complex, as the following questions will illustrate.

1. Unaccompanied choral music was most popular:
   (a) 100 years before Bach.
   (b) during the time of Bach.
   (c) 100 years after the time of Bach.

2. The breakdown of the tonal system is characterized by
   (a) increased use of chromaticism.
   (b) return to the use of modal scales.
   (c) rhythm playing an equal or greater unifying role than melody.
   (d) introduction of nontonal instruments for effects.

3. Apply the following statements to Mozart and decide whether they are true, partly true and partly false, or false.
   (a) He was the greatest musical genius the world has ever known.   T   T&F   F
   (b) He learned much from Haydn, but taught Haydn nothing.   T   T&F   F
   (c) He was less influenced by Austrian folk music than Haydn, but made greater use of chromaticism.   T   T&F   F
   (d) Weber copied much of his style in operatic overtures and arias.   T   T&F   F

1.23 Knowledge of classifications and categories. To students, classification of items may seem arbitrary and artificial, but it is the kind of knowledge the specialist makes much use of. As the student's understanding grows, he comes to find more meaning in classifying and categorizing. Such knowledge allows one to find relationships between things that on the surface may seem quite disparate.

1. Renaissance music included:

1	2	3	4
masses	masses	motets	cantatas
motets	virelais	oratorios	chansons
rondeaux	madrigals	rondeaux	chorales
chansons	antiphons	chansons	motets

2. The clarinet is considered a
   (a) brass   (b) woodwind   (c) percussion   (d) string   instrument.

1.24 Knowledge of criteria. Students should grow in their knowledge of the criteria by which an aesthetic object is judged. They should become aware that emotional reaction to a musical composition is not the sole basis for judging its worth. Included in this knowledge should be a cognizance of the sources to turn to for reliable judgment and for accurate information. Although much of the interest in criteria is at higher levels of musical learning, even small children can be given some elementary knowledge of how to go about making a sound musical judgment.

1. References are provided on a musical problem from several sources. One problem dealing with the music of Mozart is cited in four sources. Which would you consider the most authoritative?
   (a) Blume, editor, *Die Musik in Geschichte und Gegenwart: Allgemeine Enzyklopadie der Music*
   (b) Sabin editor, *International Cyclopedia of Music and Musicians*
   (c) Fetis, *Biographie Universelle des Musiciens et Bibliographie Générale de la Musique*
   (d) Ewen, *The Complete Book of Classical Music*

2. What are the two most important qualities of good singing?
   (a) correct phrasing
   (b) beautiful tone
   (c) distinct enunciation
   (d) correct breathing
   (e) accurate pitch
   (f) dynamic variety

3. The best violinist is one who:
   (a) can play fast and accurately.
   (b) has a beautiful tone.
   (c) can make the music sound the way the composer meant it to sound.
   (d) can make the music sound the way the teacher wants it to sound.

1.25 Knowledge of methodology. Methodology pertains mainly to the more advanced student. In Bloom's taxonomy, category 3.00 is application, so that the item under examination here is simple knowledge of methodology, not the use of it. Methodology is used by the performing musician, the music teacher, the music historian and researcher, and the composer and improviser.

1. Which is the proper way to produce a good attack on a wind instrument?
   (a) Scan the phrase, take a deep breath, think the pitch, and blow.
   (b) Warm up the tongue, take a deep breath, flex the lips, think the pitch, and blow.
   (c) Think the pitch, scan the phrase, take a deep breath, and blow.
   (d) Think the pitch, take enough breath to attack the note, and blow.

2. You wish to evaluate a student's ability to read music. Which would be the most valid method?

(a) Ask him to name the syllables or the names of the notes.

(b) Have him take the music home to practice then have him perform it the following day.

(c) Have him sing a number at sight from the notation.

(d) Have him play and sing the melody at the same time, using the piano.

3. From the following chord progressions, select the smoothest way to move from the key of G to the key of B. (Any pitch may be used in the soprano, and chords can be repeated.)

(a) G: I–III; B: V_7–I.

(b) G: I–VI; B: V_7–I.

(c) G: I–IV; B: V_7–I.

(d) G: I–IV; A# dim. 7th; B:I.

1.30 Knowledge of the universals and abstractions in a field.   This category pertains to the broad ideas and patterns that are used to organize and summarize the facts, events, conventions, and other phenomena in the field. Universals tend to be difficult for students to comprehend, and an adequate background in the specifics of the field is necessary to master them.

1.31 Knowledge of principles and generalizations.   Principles and generalizations help to describe or explain the most appropriate direction to be taken with a set of facts. In music, principles and generalizations may be found that pertain to teaching, to composing, to performing, to listening, and to the history of music.

1. During the process of correct breathing, an intake of breath is accompanied by

(a) expansion of the diaphragm.

(b) the shoulders rising, the chest filling with air.

(c) contraction of the diaphragm.

(d) the diaphragm remaining immobile but supporting the air pressure.

2. When we speak of the *classical principle* in music, we refer to:

(a) the belief that communication of emotion is paramount in music.

(b) the practice of writing the melodic line in the soprano with a homophonic accompaniment.

(c) attempts to imitate the music of the Greek classical period.

(d) the belief that musical expression should be contained within well-defined structures.

3. In the following list, put a "P" by each statement that represents a principle of music education.

(a) Formulate sound teaching objectives in terms of student behavior.

(b) Secure a high level of motivation.

(c) Hear many different types of music.

(d) Provide for active participation by the students.

(e) Help students grow towards musical independence.

1.32 Knowledge of theories and structures. This knowledge enables one to interrelate principles and generalizations and to understand how these fit into the larger body of a structure or a theory. It is a step beyond the previous category, where principles and generalizations are treated as particulars; here, the connections that join them are emphasized.

1. From the following statements, place an "R" by one or more statements that best exemplify Reimer's philosophy of music education. Place an "L" by one or more statements that best exemplify Leonhard's philosophy of music education. If the statement is common to both, mark "B."
   (a) Music attains significance only through its expressive appeal, and all work with music must be carried on with full cognizance of this appeal.
   (b) The music education program should be primarily aesthetic education.
   (c) Aesthetic meaning is central for music education.
   (d) Critical responses to music are nonmusical.
   (e) Music attains significance through knowing about music and through performance.
   (f) The music education program is not only aesthetic education but is also an important part of the total school program and home experiences.
   (g) The teacher should guide students' reactions to acceptable aesthetic responses determined by the aesthetic import of the music.

2. The church chant is perhaps the oldest staple of European and Western music. Write *one* sentence after each musical period named below, describing what use, if any, was made of church chant in that period.
   (a) Early Christianity, 540–750.
   (b) Franco-Flemish, 1450–1500.
   (c) Classical, 1750–1800.
   (d) Contemporary, 1913–

2.00   COMPREHENSION

Comprehension is the ability to know what is being communicated and to make some use of the facts or ideas communicated. Knowledge is based upon remembering—retention of a fact, of a convention, of a method, even of a principle or a theory. Comprehension, on the other hand, includes the objectives, behaviors, or responses that indicate an understanding of a message. Comprehension is demonstrated by ability to translate, to interpret, or to extrapolate.

2.10 Translation. Translation depends upon an adequate knowledge of the facts involved in the problem at hand. Probably the most common form of translation in music is found in the use of the musical score. If the individual can translate the score into meaningful conducting, accurate rendition in a performance, or appropriate comparisons with other scores, he displays the ability referred to in this category. A reverse kind of translation occurs when, having listened to a musical work, the individual can recognize melodic motifs and themes from the work by seeing them written in score.

1. You have been given the score for a brief musical composition. Examine the score carefully, then place an "X" beside each description that applies to the composition.

   ☐ (a) three-part form
   ☐ (b) rondo form
   ☐ (c) minuet trio form
   ☐ (d) single tonality throughout
   ☐ (e) atonal throughout
   ☐ (f) key structure of tonic, subdominant, tonic, dominant, tonic
   ☐ (g) dancelike in character
   ☐ (h) songlike in character
   ☐ (i) essentially rhythmic rather than melodic

2. Which of the following musical works most closely resembles the Mozart Requiem?
   (a) the Beethoven *Mount of Olives*
   (b) the Berlioz Requiem
   (c) the Bach B Minor Mass
   (d) the Verdi Requiem

2.20 Interpretation. Interpretation includes translation of the various parts of the problem and a comprehension of the relationships that exist between the parts. In other words, it involves the ability to locate the major elements or ideas and the knowledge of how these fit together.

1. Below are three lists showing the order of eminence in which musical critics and musicologists have placed composers in certain years. Which list shows: (a) a preference for the Romantics? (b) a preference for the Classicists?

1938	*1944*	*1951*
Bach	Bach	Beethoven
Beethoven	Beethoven	Bach
Wagner	Mozart	Brahms
Mozart	Haydn	Wagner
Palestrina	Wagner	Haydn
Haydn	Brahms	Mozart
Brahms	Palestrina	Schubert
Monteverdi	Schubert	Debussy
Debussy	Handel	Handel
Schubert	Debussy	Palestrina
Handel	Monteverdi	Monteverdi

2. The vocal music department of a large high school is making plans to present a musical-dramatic work for the public. One month is to be set aside to prepare it, using a daily hour rehearsal during school time, plus evening rehearsal for the final two weeks. Objectives for the work are as follows:

The students are to know the typical structure of a musical-dramatic work and the various subparts that make up the total work.

Students are to know a specified amount of the functional and organizational aspects of such a production.

Students are to recognize selections and match them with the appropriate operetta.

Students are to accomplish specified objectives in vocal skills and in performing skills.

Students are to learn a stipulated ability to express dramatic and narrative elements by bodily actions and by musical skills.

Examine the following list of operettas, musical comedies, and operas, and number them in the order that indicates how appropriate each is for achieving the stated objectives within the rehearsal time limits.

(a) *West Side Story,* Bernstein
(b) *Down in the Valley,* Weill
(c) *H.M.S. Pinafore,* Gilbert and Sullivan
(d) *Little Mary Sunshine,* Besoyan
(e) *Brigadoon,* Loewe

2.30 Extrapolation. To extrapolate means to extend the inferences of a communication beyond the range given in the communication. The individual uses the information to make estimates or predictions. Extrapolations may extend the given material with reference to time, to the domain or subject, or to the size of the subject matter. The following questions may help to illustrate this level of cognition.

1. In a study by Broquist on attitudes of students towards music, the students rated music higher at the second-grade level than at the sixth-grade level in comparison to their other school subjects. At each grade level the students ranked music with their other subjects of that grade level.
   (a) List three reasons that might account for this.
   (b) Assume that music is required at the junior high school level for the schools used in the Broquist study. Assume that the same kind of music situation continues at the junior high level. What results might be found from a study of the seventh- and eighth-grade attitudes in these schools?
   (c) Assume that music is not required at the junior high school level, but that in other respects the same situation continues that Broquist found to be present in the grade schools. Make at least two predictions for attitude in this situation.

2. Support for symphony orchestras in the United States is at present greater than at any time in the past. This fact is often cited as evidence that Americans are more interested in art music. The following facts are also true. Classical recordings are at an all-time high for sales. Stereo sets and high fidelity sets are at an all-time high for sales. Rock and roll, folk, and jazz recordings outsell classical recordings four to one. Twenty percent of television time is given to popular singers and recording stars, while four percent is given to opera, symphonic, chamber, or serious solo musicians.

Check below those statements that you think best explain these facts as a whole.

(a) Because music is required in the schools, students do not like classical music, and they turn to the popular forms for their listening enjoyment.

(b) Because music has been required in the schools, more people like music than ever before, some choosing classical music and some choosing popular.

(c) High incomes, increased leisure, and relative affluence have resulted in greater sales for all kinds of music, live and recorded.

(d) The population of the United States has increased, thereby producing a greater number of consumers of music.

(e) If more band and orchestra concerts were given in the schools, students would grow up wanting to attend concerts more than to stay home to watch television.

(f) If more listening were taught in the schools, students would grow up wanting to listen to classical music in concerts and on record and T.V.

(g) Public school students learn more about the music they hear on T.V. than about the music they have in school.

(h) Art music is only for those people who have natural talent and know how to understand it.

3.00 APPLICATION

Almost everything a student learns in schools is expected to have application to his out-of-school or adult life. We often believe that if an individual knows something well, he will automatically be able to apply it. Studies have shown, however, that practice is needed in transfer of training, to help the individual realize the variety of situations to which an abstract principle can apply. In music, factual knowledge is important only because it can be applied to improve skill and understanding in performing, composing, or listening. Any test for application must therefore include a musical problem or setting. Since this condition makes evaluation more difficult, the results of such testing must be examined more carefully than where straight factual knowledge is dealt with. Nevertheless, such testing is of great importance, because it duplicates the kinds of musical problems that, it is hoped, the student will elect to encounter in later life and in his out-of-school activities.

1. A flute student continually produces a breathy tone. What action would you suggest to alleviate this problem.
   (a) Lessen the opening in the embouchure.
   (b) Direct the air stream downwards more.
   (c) Practice long tones.
   (d) Check the instrument for leaks.

2. Examine the piece of music before you. State whether it is written for oboe, flute, or C trumpet. Give four reasons for your choice, citing specific characteristics of the music to support your view.

4.00 ANALYSIS

Analysis is the ability to divide some piece of cognitive material into its constituent parts in order to find relationships and organizational principles. Analysis is a familiar term in musical learning, especially at the more advanced levels of secondary school and college. In nearly every art form—poetry, music, painting, dance, etc.—analysis is used to show that one understands the elements of the work and also as a means for understanding it further. Music teaching often uses analysis as an end in itself, a kind of intellectual exercise, but it has no real value except as a means to synthesis, evaluation, or other kinds of total comprehension. Yet, problems that measure ability to analyze are useful in helping to discover whether the individual possesses this important cognitive ability.

4.10 Analysis of elements. In music, an analysis of elements might include distinguishing the instruments heard in a composition or being able to determine the number of voices or melodic lines in a work heard. The elements that make up an opera, a mass, or an oratorio might be analyzed upon hearing one of these works. The comparison of a movement from a Beethoven symphony with a movement from a Mahler symphony might illustrate the individual's grasp of the melodic and formal elements in each movement. Written harmonic analysis of chordal and formal structure from looking at the score is a common exercise in music. Such an exercise is made more valuable when some form of overview or synthesis follows the analysis.

1. Below are three versions of the same musical phrase, each version representing an arrangement for a different type of choral group. Label each vocal part in each and indicate which vocal line is the melody. [Music examples have been omitted here.]

Group 1: men's barbershop quartet
Group 2: madrigal
Group 3: antiphonal choir

4.20 Analysis of relationships. An analysis of relationships establishes some connection between the various elements and enables the individual to discover which elements are basic or foundational, which secondary or embellishing, which extraneous or perhaps misleading. For music, this ability may be illustrated by finding the germ motif upon which the musical themes of a work are based, determining the essential contours of a theme from examination of a set of variations, or examining a musical score to determine which instruments are, at any given point, playing the principal melodic lines and which the subordinate parts.

1. Follow the score of the fugue as you listen to it being played on the record. Check the correct answer below.
   (a) This is a simple fugue; the subject is presented in measures 1 and 2.
   (b) This is a fugue with a countersubject, the subject being presented in measures 1 and 2 and the countersubject occurring initially in measures 3 and 4.
   (c) This is a double fugue, the second subject occurring initially in measures 3 and 4.
   (d) This is a double fugue, the first subject occurring in measures 1 and 2, the second subject occurring in measures 76 and 77, with the two subjects combining in measure 112.

4.30 Analysis of organizational principles. Ability to analyze organizational principles means ability not only to recognize the elements and determine which are of greater and lesser importance, but also to understand how the total structure is put together. Knowledge of formal structure in music is an example of this category of cognition.

1. You will hear a composition played. Decide which of the following structures best represents the form of the work.
   (a) theme and variations
   (b) theme, development and restatement
   (c) theme 1, development; theme 2, development
   (d) introduction, theme, development[5]
2. The *theme* of the work you have just heard has which of the following formal structures:
   (a) three-phrase group, A B C
   (b) three-part form, A B A

---

[5] *Ibid.,* p. 161.

(c) three-part form A: A: B A

(d) three-part form A: A: B: B A

5.00   SYNTHESIS

Synthesis implies the putting together of elements to form a whole, and thus includes a greater element of creativity than any of the previous categories of cognition. Whereas analysis involves seeing the parts of a whole that is given, synthesis involves collecting parts from a variety of sources and putting them together into a structure. The kinds of synthesis are classified by the product, these being production of a unique communication, production of a plan of operation, and derivation of a set of abstract relations. The ability to synthesize is seen as of unique importance in education, because it indicates independence of thought and personal expression, rather than passive receptivity or purely mechanical learning. Further, problems involving synthesis offer a wider kind of experience than problems focused mainly on the acquisition of knowledge, and probably result in better retention and better ability to generalize. Although at first glance synthesis seems to be a high level ability, Bloom believes it can be taught at most levels of education. As he says, the ability to set a poem to music is an appropriate goal for grade school as well as for the Ph.D. program in music, though the complexity and magnitude of the tasks will obviously differ.[6]

5.10 Production of a unique communication. This cognitive ability can be measured by problems demanding the creation of a musical composition, with any appropriate restrictions or stipulations. For instance, a smaller child might be given a two-measure melody and asked to write two more measures that would fit those given and bring the phrase to an appropriate conclusion. Setting a simple poem to music, or creating a suitable harmony part for a melody, would also be an example of production of a unique communication. At higher levels, a specific theme might be given from which the student would compose a work within a particular form, such as theme and variations or simple rondo. A basic harmonic structure might be given; the formal structure might be the given element; an instrumental stipulation such as woodwind quintet or string trio might be the sole restriction.

5.20 Production of a plan or proposed set of operations. This ability varies from the previous one in that the unique creation involves a scheme or arrangement for doing something. The scheme itself, and not the doing, is the object of this category; the scheme or plan may not actually be carried out, or it may be carried out by someone other than

---

[6] *Ibid.,* p. 168.

the creator of the plan. This kind of problem is commonly presented to prospective teachers; the creation of a unit of instruction or even of a daily lesson plan utilizes this ability. The music student might be asked to plan materials and specific steps for teaching a particular bit of musical information such as the use of the flute in contemporary music, or meter and rhythm, or the art song. A similar problem, though with obviously less musical value, would be the creation of a football band show or the planning of an assembly program for George Washington's birthday. The selection of appropriate music for a hypothetical series of concerts might also be a measure of this ability.

5.30 Derivation of a set of abstract relations.   This ability represents a high level of cognition, which may be measured by two kinds of tasks. First, the student starts with a set of items, or phenomena, for which he must find valid relationships. Second, the student starts with a basic theory or proposition and derives subordinate principles and relations from it. As may be seen, these tasks involve none of the subjective creativity of the two previous categories, but demand a rigid attention to consistency and logical deduction. An example of the first task for music cognition might be to confront the student with an unfamiliar score, on which certain points or portions were marked. His task would be to explain the nature of each of these points, then identify the date, period, and composer of the work, and show how each of the questionable points could logically be characteristics of the composer and the period. As an illustration of the second task, the problem might be to apply a specific theory of learning, such as that of Piaget or of Bruner, to objectives of the music program, and derive activities, experiences, and appropriate measurement for a given level of learning. Setting up a valid research problem and deriving appropriate hypotheses and subproblems from the basic problem illustrate the second type task for this category.

6.00 EVALUATION

An important objective of all education is that the student become equipped to make appropriate judgments, that he learn to give consideration to all the appropriate factors related to a judgment rather than basing his evaluation on subjective or egocentric factors. Though not necessarily the highest level of cognitive activity, evaluation is placed at the end of the taxonomy because it includes use of all the other cognitive activities: knowledge, comprehension, application, analysis, and synthesis. Two kinds of judgment are included in Bloom's taxonomy: judgment in terms of internal evidence and judgment in terms of external criteria.

6.10 Judgment in terms of internal evidence. In music, as in all of the arts, accurate judgment of an item is one of the prime goals of education. To make a judgment about anything borders upon the affective domain, but as it is used here its connotation is primarily cognitive, a mentally controlled decision based upon identifiable items. Therefore, in testing for this ability, stress should be placed upon the methods employed in the judgment as much as upon the judgment itself; the student should be asked to show how and why he reached his conclusions. Internal evidence would include such items as whether the work in question is consistent or inconsistent, accurate or inaccurate, carefully or carelessly executed. For measuring this ability, questions might be framed in which the student is asked to judge the performance of a work to which he listens. The performance would need to be taped or recorded and would have to be suited to the question. The student might be given a score to follow upon which to mark the spots to support his judgments. A second kind of problem might be to evaluate a hypothetical research problem in music, or a hypothetical teaching unit, making judgments along the same types of internal characteristics as those mentioned above.

6.20 Judgments in terms of external criteria. This activity differs from the above category in that the thing being judged is examined in terms of utility, appropriateness, or efficiency. The student must know both the characteristics of the thing he is examining and the criteria required by the particular situation. For example, a problem might be to inspect several musical works or musical activities that are to be used to teach a specific kind of musical knowledge. The student must decide upon the appropriateness and effectiveness of each of these musical works for that goal. In making his decisions, he shows his mastery of learning psychology and of the requirements for that specific musical knowledge, and his understanding of the musical works and their possible utility. Other problems might focus upon the evaluation of a scholarly article, of a textbook, of an aesthetic theory to be applied to learning situations, or of a set of objectives for the music curriculum.

In illustrating various ways to measure cognitive ability, the preceding pages have offered numerous examples of test questions. It is hoped that the teacher will find these useful in creating his own tests of cognition. Careful attention to the taxonomy may prevent omission of certain levels of cognitive development, both in evaluation and in planning. Several good publications exist that contain extensive illustrations of possible test items, among which is *Specimen Objective Test Items* by Gerberich.[7]

---

[7] J. Raymond Gerberich, *Specimen Objective Test Items: A Guide to Achievement Test Construction* (New York: Longmans, Green and Co. Ltd., 1956).

OTHER EVALUATIVE DEVICES

In addition to the objective test, outside assignments of all kinds have traditionally been used as one of the bulwarks of cognitive evaluation. These are probably more important for learning than for evaluating, but the two go hand in hand. An outside assignment should be related to classwork. It should have a genuine focus in learning so that it is more than busywork. Above all, it must be graded and the grade recorded by the teacher, for one problem of outside assignments in music has been that so often they are not used in any meaningful way. The student soon learns that assignments will not be asked for or will not be carefully studied by the teacher. In such cases, their value is lost.

Pictorial items such as identification of instruments or of kinds of musical groups are not limited in their usefulness to small children. A portion of a score, for example, may be displayed by means of an opaque projector and the class asked to tell as much about it as they can—when written, style, intended for what group, possible composer, possible form, melodic motifs, chords used, and other analytical information. A listening test with similar instructions, where students hear the work rather than see it, is also a kind of pictorial item, an aural picture rather than a visual one.

Essay tests remain a very valuable device for evaluation when carefully constructed and carefully graded. Checklists may be used to aid objectivity. For example, written work could be rated according to the following outline:

Quality and quantity of investigation of topic.

Limited investigation			*Fair*			*Extensive**		
1	2	3	1	2	3	1	2	3

Form and style.

Poor use of words			*Fair usage*			*Good, cogent style**		
1	2	3	1	2	3	1	2	3

Any other items that are deemed important can be included, for example, organization or focus upon the elements of major importance. Open-book tests have similar qualities: their use in motivation and in

---

* Descriptive words lack objectivity but when coupled with a numerical scale and used as only one device in a comprehensive evaluation program, they do provide information.

learning is high, and when questions are skillfully contrived they can be a fairly accurate guide to how well the student knows the material and how well he is able to put together ideas and facts to solve a problem. For many kinds of learning it is more important to assess the student's ability to find and understand information than it is to test his retention of knowledge.

Diagnostic tests are similar to achievement tests, differing primarily in use. With a diagnostic test, part scores and perhaps individual questions are examined in search of problem areas that are giving difficulty to the students. Standardized tests having sections that may be used for diagnostic work are the Aliferis, Aliferis-Stecklein, Snyder-Knuth, and Colwell *Musical Achievement Tests*. These have relatively good reliability with part scores, although the Snyder-Knuth test is not organized to provide information on parts. A teacher-constructed diagnostic test would contain questions on only one specific area; the results would not be considered as achievement scores and thus would not be reflected by course grades. Both achievement and diagnostic tests are classified as mastery tests.

One of the greatest dangers of objective measurement in the cognitive domain is attempting to cover too many subjects and too much information in one test, thus measuring so many kinds of cognitive abilities that the results are not helpful. Concentration upon a relatively narrow area of knowledge or upon a clearly defined set of abilities will produce a test that gives more information useful to the teacher in further planning and teaching.

QUESTIONS FOR DISCUSSION

1. Discuss the most important cognitive objectives for each level of the taxonomy in music education.
2. Identify different methods of evaluation and create sample questions for each level of the taxonomy.
3. What level of the taxonomy would be most appropriate when considering objectives for high school performing groups?

REFERENCES

Bloom, Benjamin, ed., *Taxonomy of Educational Objectives: The Classification of Educational Goals, Handbook 1: Cognitive Domain.* New York: David McKay Co., Inc., 1956, Chapter 6.

Wood, Dorothy Adkins, *Test Construction: Development and Interpretation of Achievement Tests.* Columbus, Ohio: Charles E. Merrill Books, Inc., 1961, Appendices B and C.

CHAPTER SIX

evaluating musical skills

PSYCHOMOTOR ABILITIES

This chapter is concerned with the development and evaluation of psychomotor abilities. *Psychomotor* suggests that motion—activity, skills, physical accomplishment—results from the combination of mind and body, the mind sending the signal to the hand, foot, or face to perform some task. Without the mind, the body will not develop skills; even though the term is shortened to motor skills the mind is still the controlling element. However, some individuals have better physical equipment for the performance of certain skills—greater strength, greater dexterity, longer legs, or broader hands, which help them become more skillful than individuals not so equipped. Therefore, both mind and body are vital for the development of skills, though some skills are largely mental and some more predominantly physical.

In the academic world, motor skills do not receive the same measure of respect as do cognitive abilities. The mark of the educated person has been his command of facts and his ability to think, with skills recognized only as they aid the performance of cognitive tasks. Music performance falls well within the definition of a skill, being far more a psychomotor activity than a cognitive one. Musicians generally have been given little status unless their skills were so highly developed as to make them unique—the virtuoso artist or the assemblage of a number of virtuosi into a string quartet or a symphony orchestra. The tendency to think of music as a trade has been tacitly accepted by the American educational system. In large city systems that offer specialized programs for the musically gifted, the program is often located in the vocational high school so that it does not conflict with the college preparatory curriculum of the other high schools. The music conservatory is designed to help budding professional musicians avoid the requirements of liberal education and to allow more time for polishing skills to an even higher sheen. Public and private colleges try to compete with the conservatory; a maximum of skill courses is offered and eagerly sought by the music students, while all effort is made to keep the cognitive courses to a minimum. with even that minimum resented by students who yearn for more time to practice or play in performing groups.

Unfortunately, skill development has not been considered a basic part of public school education, or at least not on a par with cognitive development. To quote Bloom, ". . . we find so little done about it (skill development) in secondary schools or colleges, that we do not believe the development of a classification of (skill) objectives would be very useful at the present."[1] With this situation in force, it is not surprising that little need has been felt for a systematic evaluation program in public school music. When skills are considered something subsidiary and specialized, not applicable to all, little thought is given to whether the program is fulfilling its expected objectives.

NEW TRENDS

The role of skills in the education of children seems to have altered somewhat in recent years. Physical education personnel took the lead when they decided that physical activity was beneficial to all students and that one need not make the first team to be eligible for these benefits. A campaign was conducted to convince educators and lay people of the need for a program broader than skill development for competition, a program that contributed to each student in terms of health, recreation, and appreciation. The stars of the football and basketball teams were not excused from the new physical education courses; rather, the de-

---

[1] Benjamin Bloom, ed., *Taxonomy of Educational Objectives, Handbook I: Cognitive Domain* (New York: David McKay Co., Inc., 1956), pp. 7–8.

velopment of athletes was seen as one outgrowth of the new broad program for all.

In music, where performance has for so long been the primary focus, a similar trend is evolving. Performing groups continue to dominate, but general courses have been added to the music program. The objectives for the performing groups have changed from performance for its own sake—winning contests and giving concerts—to performance as a vehicle for appreciation. The new objectives are often more real to the writers of the new philosophies than to the band, orchestra, and chorus teacher, but in any event, the emphasis has shifted to instruction. The teacher is aware of his obligation to all the students in his groups or his classes, to teach musical skills because they apply to either appreciation or performance, and to teach as many performing skills as the situation will allow. Plainly, the teacher is more conscious of the broad possibilities of his field, although it is difficult to find ways to teach both appreciation and performance, to develop both audience and artist, using the same curriculum. Even to list musical skills and performing skills is a formidable task; in the following pages a number of such skills will be specified with suggestions made for evaluating each at various levels of development. Because musicianship is made up of such a variety of skills, the only way to estimate student progress is to evaluate many of these skills periodically for each student.

A TAXONOMY OF PSYCHOMOTOR OBJECTIVES

Skills range from acts that are almost entirely motor, such as digging with a shovel, to acts that are almost entirely mental, such as aural perception of sounds. A system is needed to discuss skills in terms of relationships, difficulty, and use. Despite Bloom's opinion that a taxonomy of the psychomotor domain was of little use to schools, Elizabeth Simpson has developed a tentative classification system, which she believes to be hierarchical in nature and which parallels Krathwohl's taxonomy for the affective domain.[2] Simpson's system is helpful as a means of organizing musical skills, but it cannot be followed rigidly; so little is known about the nature of aural skills and how they develop that it is unwise to accept Simpson's taxonomy as representing a genuine hierarchy. Actually, each major classification of musical skill seems to follow a cyclical structure through which growth takes place from simple to complex.

---

[2] Elizabeth Simpson, *The Classification of Educational Objectives, Psychomotor Domain*, final report, U.S. Office of Education Contract # 5-85-104 (Urbana, Illinois: College of Education, University of Illinois, 1966).

Evaluation must be made of each aspect of skill development. Obviously there must be many specific skill objectives, all of them worked for, to insure well-balanced growth. There must then also be many specific evaluations to determine progress toward the variety of objectives. One of the errors of music has been to wait for evaluation of skills until the performer is somewhat advanced. This practice makes evaluation easier, but it fails to help improve instruction at the earlier stages. To make an analogy with academic subjects, this would be comparable to waiting until the student started high school to evaluate his reading or computational ability. At this level, it is often too late to take corrective measures, and the student falls by the wayside. Such a practice is not only unfair but positively harmful, yet it has continued for many years in music with little thought given to the music program's responsibility for the individual student and his training. The only way to meet this responsibility is to continually observe the student as skills develop. Simpson's taxonomy of psychomotor skills is as follows:

1.0 *Perception:* the process of becoming aware of objects, qualities, or relations by use of the sense organs.
   1.1 *Sensory stimulation:* impingement of a stimulus upon one or more of the sense organs.
   1.2 *Cue selection:* deciding what cues to respond to in meeting the requirements of a task (ability to distinguish among sensory stimuli).
   1.3 *Translation:* determining the meaning of the cues for action.

2.0 *Set:* preparatory adjustment or readiness for a particular kind of action or experience.
   2.1 *Mental set:* readiness to perform a motor act (knowledge of).
   2.2 *Physical set:* having made the anatomical adjustments necessary for a motor act.
   2.3 *Emotional set:* readiness in terms of favorable attitude.

3.0 *Guided response:* overt behavioral action under the guidance of an instructor.
   3.1 *Imitation:* execution of an act in response to another person performing the act.
   3.2 *Trial and error:* trying various responses until an appropriate response is achieved.

4.0 *Mechanism:* the learned response has become habitual.

5.0 *Complex overt response:* smooth and efficient performance of a complex motor act.
   5.1 *Resolution of uncertainty:* knowledge of the sequence; proceeding with confidence.
   5.2 *Automatic performance:* ability to perform a finely coordinated motor skill with much ease and muscle control.

6.0   *Adaptation:* ability to change a performance to make it more suitable.

7.0   *Origination:* ability to develop new skills.

A translation of the taxonomy in terms of musical skills appears in Appendix A. However, much value can be gained from a class assignment to organize and evaluate musical skills using the taxonomy as a guide.

EVALUATING SKILLS IN A MUSICAL SETTING

The comment is sometimes made that musical instruction cannot be clinically approached in the manner suggested by the use of a taxonomy. To analyze the factors in musical skills and focus upon them one at a time is to destroy the essence of the musical experience, which is an entity greater than the sum of its parts, so the belief goes. True, perhaps. Therefore, most of the clinical analysis should be done by the teacher, who in planning total music experiences for his students must also plan for their total musical growth. In order to accomplish the latter, he will have to employ some objective scrutiny both of his students' skills and of his own teaching objectives. A widely influential learning theory advocates the cycle of synthesis-analysis-synthesis, where after the broad and encompassing experience the learner is given the chance to dissect and examine that experience in detail before he returns again, enriched, to the broad experience. Most of the objections to the analytical approach may be traced to a distaste for the old fashioned "European" mode of private instruction, in which the student was subjected only to the detail, the dissecting, the analysis of technique, the continual drill upon exercises and études, until he had acquired sufficient skill for the master to allow him to make music with genuine compositions. To believe that such is the viewpoint of the present book is a grave misinterpretation. Truly, the public school music program might profit by some seasoning from the old masters' approach, but the meat of the program must continue to be experiences that will broaden and enrich, not confine or restrict. As important as clinical evaluation is, it must be augmented by evaluation of skills as these are assembled in the act of making music.

GENERAL PERFORMANCE EVALUATION

Concerts and Contests

Concerts, festivals, and contests are excellent means of evaluation. Individuals can be evaluated through solo appearances with a group, through leadership positions such as first chair in the section, through recital appearances, and through solo performance at contests. Small groups may be observed as they accompany a soloist, as featured sections in a composition for concert, through small ensemble concerts, in ensemble performances at contests, and at performances for local civic groups of all kinds.

In order to retain real evaluative benefit from a performance situation, the setting must be structured. Evaluation of a concert usually consists of the opinions of concerned but perhaps unenlightened parents, the exhilaration of the stimulated performers, and the reactions of the exhausted conductor. The music contest provides a structure for evaluation. When the contest judges are competent and conscientious and are not forced into too crowded a schedule, their comments can be the most meaningful evaluation of performance the student receives. Outside evaluation is important not only for the junior high school orchestra but also for the polished professional group. One of the concerns of professional musicians in residence away from major cities is that their performance standards slip when they are without the judgments of professional critics for an extended period. Many orchestras arrange tours to New York City, and solo artists schedule Carnegie Hall or Town Hall concerts, because they know they need the opinions of the critics in order to maintain the highest performing standards. All performers need a similar outside evaluation as feedback to improve the learning process. This type of evaluation is judgmental; no text can predict whether criticism at a contest will be adequate, sound, or sufficiently thoroughgoing to offer the value one hopes to receive from it. A single contest for the public school band is like one criticism of a New York performance. The judgments may not be valid, they may be based on too little evidence, but they are realistic, for performing skills in all areas are judged on a single display—one concert, one solo, one recital. If the skills are not reliable enough to depend upon during the pressure of public performance, then they are inadequate, and more rigorous training is required before the next performance. Judgments concerning the musicality of a performance are more complex, but the performer must be skillful enough to express his musical ideas, since this is the only way they are communicated. In the teaching situation, then, it is imperative that situations are offered in which adequate outside judgments are given, and where students gain confidence in performing for critics.

The practice of asking one or more judges to attend each performance during the year and to submit written comments can be helpful. With younger groups and soloists the judges may be given some structure for evaluation in order to conform to the instructional level. With older, more advanced players, more freedom may be given the critic, though this is not always desirable. If concerts are really to be learning devices, qualified colleagues and private teachers should be glad to offer helpful comments and make thoughtful suggestions rather than to give the customary plaudits and gratuities of polite people. The request-criticism situation need not be limited to concerts, although performance is usually at its peak then. Evaluation by the conductor's peers is valid at contests, rehearsals, and at festivals.

Students, if properly taught, can also make appropriate judgments on skills. Students from neighboring schools and from other performing groups within a school can make judgments without becoming negative if they themselves have experienced evaluation as an aid rather than as a threat. Teachers who enlist student decisions on membership and chair placement find that young players have sound judgment and a great desire to be fair. Peer evaluation is often even more severe than that which a teacher would offer, but it can be just as constructive. Performance evaluation should not be neglected by the elementary and general music teachers. The teaching of classroom singing and performing skills can be evaluated in the same manner, only with modified standards.

Another successful method of evaluation is to employ a professional performer to work with a group for a short period of time, three days or a week, with or without a culminating concert. No conductor can be an outstanding technician on all instruments or equally versed in the problems of all voice types. A recognized professional can augment the teacher's strengths and can view the status of the group and the individuals from a different perspective. Two benefits may be expected from the evaluation offered by such an individual. First, he can make criticisms that the teacher may have omitted and help to correct oversights and errors in the learning. Second, he can reinforce the teacher's criticisms and evaluations, since students are inclined to be impressed with the words of the recognized expert. What the visiting professional says is taken to be the word of truth and his opinions are heeded, collected, and repeated for weeks.

Exchange concerts with comparable schools or comparable groups offer opportunities for evaluation. These can be less formal and less demanding than the public concert, having as their primary purpose cross-criticism between conductors and students. As with any student participation in evaluation, the bases for criticism need to be carefully delineated so that there is a positive rather than a negative result from the effort. When this is accomplished, the students learn not only from what members of the other group have to say about them, but also from the careful listening and thinking they are required to do in making a fair evaluation of the other group.

A practice often found among good private teachers is that of holding a student at his lesson for a few moments to perform for the next student. This has great value for motivation as well as evaluation and is one of the fundamental advantages of class piano instruction. In addition, it helps the student to overcome his nervousness when confronted by listeners. Similar activities can be helpful with performing groups where feasible. Sections, chamber groups, soloists, perhaps even spontaneously organized groups should be heard and evaluated by their peers as well as by the teacher.

In student evaluation as well as in teacher evaluation, the problem is to focus attention on the proper things. A short evaluation form for each of the major skill areas may be kept in all of the music folders, so that when an opportunity arises to gain peer criticism for an individual or a group, there will be an outline to follow. Lacking this, the teacher may quickly sketch such an outline on the board. If this is not done, some listeners will be influenced by the performer's posture, others by his left hand technique, his bowing, the tone quality he produces, or even by the fact that he is tall, broad-shouldered, and handsome. The variety of skills is so numerous that random listening can be not only wasteful but even harmful, because the wrong conclusions are reached.

SECTION REHEARSALS

The section rehearsal presents an excellent opportunity for the teacher to evaluate performing skills. Performance is carefully observed, errors corrected, improvements suggested and tried, with a resulting increase in skill, however slight. Because the group is small, the teacher has a better chance of observing individuals than in the full rehearsal. To make the task easier, the sectional may be led by a student so that the teacher is free to observe and record individual strengths and weaknesses.

RECORDING DEVICES

Audio and video tape recorders were mentioned in the earlier part of the chapter. The advantages of replay are obvious: the tapes may be played at leisure where the environment is more conducive to thoughtful observation than in the hurry of the classroom rehearsal or lesson; students and outside experts, as well as the teacher, can observe; the tapes may be replayed as often as necessary.

Video tapes offer the chance to watch set and mechanism in skill development, and even the audio tapes reveal much that is overlooked in class and lesson. Many performing organizations make records for public sale. When this is desirable, it can be used as an excellent experience in learning through evaluation, as the process of taping, listening, and taping again for a polished performance takes place.

Hearing their own performance, be it a musical item played or sung or a spoken answer to a thought question, reveals much to students. They hear mistakes of which they were unaware; points that the teacher has been emphasizing for weeks are brought home. Conductors who use tape recorders in rehearsal report that parts of the music that sounded good during rehearsal may actually have had serious flaws. Skillful listening and an objective view are required to evaluate any performance, but especially that of one's own class or organization. In addition, it is easier to listen for something specific such as wrong notes or poor balance than to be alert to all flaws of whatever nature.

A form for writing down reactions as one listens can be put to good use both in teacher evaluation of the tapes and in student evaluation. A few points should be emphasized at a time. The best results from the tape recorder occur when it is used periodically throughout the year; evaluation of any kind must be continuous if it is to be meaningful.

The video tape recorder offers all the advantages of the tape recorder plus the advantage of seeing visual causes of performance assets and defects. Embouchure, bow arm, hand position, and posture are all caught for the viewer to behold and evaluate. One or two items should be isolated for study at each viewing, for the performing process is so complex that careful attention to sound distracts from attention to sight, and vice versa. The video tape has the disadvantages of the tape recorder—some trouble is involved in setting it up and listening to it afterwards—and with the video tape recorder the inconveniences are enlarged. The great advantage of both devices is that they can repeat the identical process for several evaluators, so that the subjectivity of a single evaluator can be overcome. One example of an evaluation form to accompany video tape viewing is given below.

TV SELF-RATING SHEET FOR CONDUCTING

Date: _____

Name: _____   Composition: _____

Score each item by circling numbers at left. 5 = outstanding; 4 = excellent; 3 = acceptable, could be improved; 2 = somewhat weak, needs considerable improvement; 1 = very weak, needs much improvement

A. 5 4 3 2 1 *General Manner* (confident, authoritative, energetic, positive)
B. 5 4 3 2 1 *Posture* (erect, relaxed, confident, commanding)
C. 5 4 3 2 1 *Starting Position* (commanding, easily visible, positive); maintained distinctive movement

D. 5 4 3 2 1   *Visual Contact* (not score-bound, especially at opening)
E. 5 4 3 2 1   *Beginning* (together, in tempo, good dynamic level, spirit)
F. 5 4 3 2 1   *Baton Technique* (correct pattern, character, size, position)
G. 5 4 3 2 1   *Clarity* (pulsation clear, definite, regular, commanding)
H. 5 4 3 2 1   *Cues* (adequate number, effectiveness, clarity, accuracy)
 I. 5 4 3 2 1   *Balance* (attention shifts among prominent sections, supportive)
 J. 5 4 3 2 1   *Left Hand* (reserved for special effects, cueing, dynamics)
K. 5 4 3 2 1   *Phrasing* (shape not ignored, nuance, variability of beat size, speed)
L. 5 4 3 2 1   *Facility* (graceful, well-coordinated, accurate)
M. 5 4 3 2 1   *Efficiency* (size and energy of beat appropriate, no excess)
N. 5 4 3 2 1   *Dynamics* (markings observed, good taste indicated)
O. 5 4 3 2 1   *Accuracy* (general freedom from conducting errors)
P. 5 4 3 2 1   *Expressiveness* (interpretation, feeling, freedom, musicianship)
Q. 5 4 3 2 1   *Tempo* (appropriate for expressive character, marking observed)
R. 5 4 3 2 1   *Ensemble* (rhythmic unity, articulative unity, neatness)
S. 5 4 3 2 1   *Quality* (intonation, tone quality, balance, unity)
T. 5 4 3 2 1   *How well did the group follow your conducting?*
U. 5 4 3 2 1   *Score Study* (detailed, thorough, well fixed in mind)
                    (Be as honest as possible with yourself on this point.)
V. 5 4 3 2 1   *Individual Practice* (with tape, other recording, conducting own singing of parts of the score, anticipating difficulties)
                    (Again, be honest with yourself.)
W. 5 4 3 2 1   *Overall Conducting Effectiveness*

DEMONSTRATIONS

Student demonstrations, either planned or informal, can be used frequently with good effect. Demonstrations occur on the spur of the moment when the instructor asks an individual or a section to illustrate the correct performance of a melodic passage, a rhythmic pattern, a scale, or a chord structure. Planned demonstrations of technique, tone, or timbre can be given for the group, for another music class, for a classroom of small children, or as a recruiting device for all performing organizations. All of these offer effective opportunities for motivation and learning as well as for evaluation. The teacher should carefully observe these situations and record his reactions objectively.

Students enjoy and profit from the preparation of a planned demonstration, and the spontaneous approach helps keep them prepared. Students can be allowed to judge themselves. They learn a good deal by deciding what aspects of performance or knowledge should be rated and by conscientiously attempting to give a valid rating. The teacher can learn about both the performers and the judges through this process. Some evaluators feel that students should not be expected to make judgments of great consistency but agree that with a skillful teacher it can be a helpful activity.

To increase objectivity, scorecards can be made for musical performance of any kind. These are used to tabulate errors, since tabulation of correct items would be neither feasible nor useful in improving performance. For scoring violin performance one might find:

Left hand position and use:	good	fair	poor
Errors	1–2	2–7	8 or more
Body position:	good	fair	poor
Errors	1	2	3

This kind of tabulation is useful for beginning classes of any kind—singing, music reading, or playing—in which short-range objectives are set up and progress is measured. At levels of greater advancement, some sort of rating scale with weighted values (some items receiving more points than others) would be appropriate. The point is that any specific list with specific answers to check or circle can improve evaluation by adding the much-needed element of objectivity.

AUDITIONS

Tryouts, auditions, and challenges for chair placement are forms of evaluation familiar to most instrumental and some vocal groups. These are more beneficial to learning, as well as more objective, when a uniform tool such as a checklist is used for evaluation. The same checklist may be used at the end of the year so that both instructor and student see the improvement in skill.

LESSONS

Private lessons given by the instructor are probably the most common and the most reliable method for evaluating individual performance skills. The elements of the private lesson should be kept in mind by the public school teacher, because the one-to-one relationship of teacher and student produces effective results, some of which can be achieved in group situations if the teacher uses the proper methods. Evaluation in the private lesson is subjective, but this is balanced by the quantity of evaluations made. The private lesson is a continual evaluation: the student performs a warm-up, and the teacher points out various ways he can improve it or uses it to teach him some facts about music and musical construction; he performs a composition he has practiced, and the teacher again evaluates, criticizes, and analyzes, demonstrating to make his points and asking the student to imitate the teacher's performance or follow the teacher's instructions. This goes on for the length of the lesson, through various kinds of materials, at various stages of perfection, and representing various kinds of learnings: cognitive, psychomotor, and affective. The student knows what the teacher wants, and he aims for that goal. The teacher concentrates upon finding the specific points that seem to need improvement and also those points upon which he can commend the student. At the close of the lesson, the student has a feeling of achievement if he deserves it and knows what to practice for the next lesson. All of these characteristics can and should be part of the group situation, though not for every student at every class meeting.

TOOLS FOR EVALUATING PSYCHOMOTOR SKILLS

It cannot be emphasized too much that casual, superficial observation often leads to erroneous conclusions, which hinder rather than aid the learning process. Observations must be made in terms of individuals rather than for group conclusions. When evaluations are made in terms of sections or ensembles (the sopranos can't produce a good tone above F sharp, the second clarinets are continually flat, the trombones this year are poor sight-readers), the objective is no longer individual skill development but production of the best total effect. In order to accomplish individual evaluation, some tools or aids that are uniform for all students and that make possible specific statements about skills must be used.

CHECKLISTS AND RATING SCALES

One such tool is the checklist. The list may be used for any type of skill evaluation and may contain whatever features the teacher feels to be desirable for that skill. For instrumentalists, some items might include tone, articulation, pitch accuracy, embouchure, finger position, fingering patterns, and dexterity. Many such forms are easily available. The MENC publishes a NIMAC (National Interscholastic Music Activities Commission) sheet, and state contests usually have forms of their own. Checklists may be used by teachers to rate adequate coverage of objectives, of pedagogical tasks, or of routine details. Checklists may be used by the student himself to evaluate his progress in performance, his study habits, or his acquisition and use of knowledge. Checklists may be used by students to evaluate their peers, by teachers to evaluate students, or by students or outsiders rating the teacher. A checklist may be used as a guide for listening to recorded or live music. Preparing the checklist is often as valuable as using it, for one becomes sensitive to the proper sequence of things and to relationships between items. To be of greatest value, the checklist should be drawn up with definite goals in mind. Some items may be appropriate for membership auditions but may not be needed in chair placement tryouts during the school year. The checklist may be designed to evaluate technical facility alone; it may be for the purpose of examining general musicianship. It may deal with music reading or with practiced performance. Another way to help make the checklist useful is to mark evaluations upon a point scale, for example, 1 to 10, the lowest number indicating extremely poor and the highest indicating completely satisfactory. Descriptive words such as poor, good, excellent, and superior are usually subjective and must be used with care. Good may mean good in comparison to others who auditioned, good for a beginning player, good as compared with all of the members of the chorus, or just good. If at the end of the year the performer is still rated good in that particular item, he will not know whether he has made progress or whether he is just where he was. Numbers can also be used subjectively, of course, but more careful thinking is involved when a wide range of numbers is used. When the evaluation is repeated at a later date, it will be easier to show progress by the increase of one or two points, but still indicating that much room for improvement remains.

Rating scales are fairly sophisticated scorecards, enabling an accurate reporting of the quality of the learning being observed. Rating scales take considerable preparation if they are to adequately cover each element of an act. After they have been created, however, they are usable in many situations and for different groups of students. Only a single aspect of performance or a single element of understanding should be covered by one rating item. For example, intonation might be rated as follows:

1	2	3
poor	*average*	*good*
Most pitches inaccurate; few can be recognized within a quarter tone	Some pitches are missed, usually only the more difficult such as large intervals or unusual skips.	Most pitches are accurate; student is rarely out of tune.

Comment (supplied by teacher): Student seems to have a poor ear.

Tone quality:

Thin, pinched, not properly supported	Some good tone but not consistent	Full, pleasant sound, appropriate for instrument

1	2	3	4	5	6	7	8	9

The descriptive words only aid in helping the teacher find an appropriate numerical rating for each person being rated.

Examples of tools for skill evaluation are difficult to present and may be misleading because their content depends almost solely upon teacher objectives and the skill level of the student. Further, the relative importance of items within a skill category, for example, technique, change depending upon the ability of the student. At one stage of sight-reading, accuracy of notes might be of greatest concern; at a more advanced stage the notes are less important than ability to properly interpret the musical style at sight. Therefore, in any aspect of skill evaluation, objective determination of the items to be observed and their weight is necessary before observing. For example, if one were to prepare a skill evaluation form for sight-reading, the first step would be to formulate appropriate items for the situation, such as:

> accuracy of pitch reading
> accuracy of rhythmic reading
> tone production
> observation of score markings
> proper musical interpretation

Then the weight of each item for this level of skill development would be determined:

> accuracy of pitch reading, 25 percent
> accuracy of rhythm reading, 25 percent
> tone production, 10 percent
> observation of score markings, 15 percent
> proper musical interpretation, 25 percent

The evaluator might wish to further subdivide these categories to aid in consistency of judgment. He might want to observe the player's confidence, as exhibited by his performance of attacks, releases, and tone production. The next step is to devise a rating scale for each item to be considered. These are usually 5-, 7-, or 9-point scales ranging from poor to excellent.

		5	
accuracy of note reading	25%	1 9
accuracy of rhythm reading	25%	1 9
(etc.)			

Each degree of objectivity helps reduce the possibilities of the rater being influenced unduly by one factor, such as the looks of the student, his manner, or his ability in a single aspect of sight-reading.

Two checklists published by the National Interscholastic Music Activities Commission are shown here. Rather than a point scale, the letters A through E are used. The form does not indicate whether all items are equal in weight; this is something that the teacher may wish to decide depending upon objectives and the skill level of students.

BAND

Order or time of appearance _____ Event No. _____ Class _____ Date _____ 19 __

Name of Organization _____

School _____ Number of Players _____

City _____ State _____ District _____ School Enrollment _____

Selections _____

_____

_____

Adjudicator will grade principal items A, B, C, D, or E, or numerals, in the respective squares. Comments must deal with fundamental principles and be constructive. Minor details may be marked on music furnished to adjudicator.

TONE (beauty, blend, control) _____ ☐

_____

INTONATION (chords, melodic line, tutti) _____ ☐

_____

TECHNIQUE (articulation, facility, precision, rhythm) _____ ☐

_____

BALANCE (ensemble, sectional) _____ ☐

_____

INTERPRETATION (expression, phrasing, style, tempo) _____ ☐

_____

MUSICAL EFFECT (artistry, fluency) _____ ☐

_____

OTHER FACTORS (choice of music, instrumentation, discipline, appearance) _____

_____

_____

* May be continued on other side

Signature of Adjudicator _____

- -

Adjudicator's private comments for _____, to be detached by
(name of Director)
adjudicator and sealed in attached envelope furnished by Festival Chairman

(Use reverse side for additional comments)

VOCAL SOLO

Order or time of appearance _____ Event No. _____ Class _____ Date _____ 19 __

Name _____ _____ Voice Classification _____

School _____

City _____ State _____ District _____

Selections _____ _____

_____

_____

Adjudicator will grade principal items A, B, C, D, or E, or numerals, in the respective squares. Comments must deal with fundamental principles and be constructive. Minor details may be marked on music furnished to adjudicator.

TONE (beauty, control) _____ ☐

INTONATION _____ ☐

DICTION (clarity of consonants, naturalness, purity of vowels) _____ ☐

TECHNIQUE (accuracy of notes, breathing, posture, rhythm) _____ ☐

INTERPRETATION (expression, phrasing, style, tempo) _____ ☐

MUSICAL EFFECT (artistry, fluency, vitality) _____ ☐

OTHER FACTORS (choice of music, stage presence and appearance) _____ ☐

* May be continued on other side

Signature of Adjudicator _____

Additional scales are available from NIMAC for sight-reading, orchestra, student conductor, marching band, twirling, solos, and so on.

The following skills evaluation chart is from the University of Illinois String Research Project. It uses a nine-point scale, plus a description of the skill to be evaluated, which aids in focusing the evaluator's attention on the skill and perhaps helps in maintaining a set standard. In addition to the written description, photographs that show each item to be observed have also been used on the evaluation chart.

UNIT TWO: EVALUATION CRITERIA AND FORM

1. Early bow hold with help of left hand.   1 2 3 4 5 6 7 8 9

    Hold the bow above the frog but not above the balance point. The thumb and little finger must be curved, the hair close to the thumb. At first, the left hand helps to steady the bow at tip.

    Comments:

2. Shuttle (middle-high).   1 2 3 4 5 6 7 8 9

    The violin is well placed, high enough on the shoulder so that the student can slide up to the top position. The tip of the thumb aids in balancing the instrument at the throat of the neck. When in the high position the fingers are extended and almost straight in the highest position. The student can shift back and forth without shaking the violin or relocating it on the shoulder. Do this first with right hand help, then without. Pluck and strum in the middle and high positions.

    Comments:

3. Shuttle: match, stopped, and harmonic octaves.   1 2 3 4 5 6 7 8 9

    The student plays octaves with 0–3 fingering alternately with 0–4 (harmonic) on the same string. The tone of the harmonic is acceptable, and the fingered octave is in tune. (The strings must be tuned well.)

Comments:

After listening to several students perform, the teacher often loses his ability to judge objectively. All begin to sound the same and to be rated the same. This is a common occurrence in the general music classroom. One solution is to force the attention of the evaluator by requiring discriminations to be made regardless of sample size. One method of forced discrimination would be to rate students by predetermined categories. For example, if one were evaluating ten clarinet players on tonguing, the evaluator would be required to rate the players against each other: one player would be rated best of the group, two above average, four average, two below average, and one poorest, even though the differences among the ten might be small. This aids in maintaining an equitable rating throughout the year and avoids what often happens with subjective judgments, that all are rated poor in the fall and all seem acceptable by spring. Forced discrimination can be used to evaluate any skill the teacher desired.

Another method, which uses the present group level of performance as a standard, does not force a specific number of students into categories but rather insures the proper use of the term "average." If the teacher feels comfortable with the old-fashioned method of grading between 70 and 100, he should determine the midpoint, 85 as average, rating half the class above 85 and half below. The usual expectations would be that most of those above average in the particular skill development being evaluated would receive scores between 85 and 95, with very few scores above this point. Similarly, most students below the average *of this particular class* would receive scores between 75 and 85. This method of evaluation will become meaningful and easy to use once the teacher is able to disassociate numerical evaluation and grades.

There is practically no limit to the type and format of rating scales that can be devised:

excellent technique	sluggish
exact articulation	sloppy
true pitch	out of tune

The precise wording of the scale is not as important as that each term has precise meaning for the teacher and can be converted to a quantitative rating.

Charts on each student's development can be used:

tone quality	very bad	bad	fair	good	very good	not consistent	lack of talent
articulation							
sight-reading							
aural perception							
pitch accuracy							

Sometimes used are checklists that avoid making a value judgment but describe competency as being either present or absent:

Constructs	A	B	C	D	E	F	Student G	H
initiative								
musicianship								
technique								
industry								

Charts may be used for the entire group or for each student. Just how they are used depends upon objectives and methods.

AURAL AND AUDITORY VISUAL TOOLS

Graded exercises can be constructed or assembled to measure various aspects of skill development. One area that has received attention from test makers is sight singing and sight-reading. Sight-reading tests are fairly easy to construct. The teacher must find music that is unfamiliar to the student and that can be graded according to several levels of difficulty. The drawback with teacher-constructed tests is that there is no standard for comparison of student achievement with other students across the nation; if the teacher is weak in teaching sight-reading, no indication of this can be gleaned from the local norms. A measure to test reading skills for the trumpet player was developed by John Watkins,[3] psychologist at the University of Montana. This test, the product of careful research, has been adapted by Farnum[4] for all wind and string instruments. National norms are available. The scoring process is difficult, because each error in note, rhythm, time, dynamics, phrasing, and accent must be marked if an accurate evaluation is desired. The norming of the Watkins-Farnum test was neither rigorously controlled nor random, but

---

[3] John Watkins, *Objective Measurement of Instrumental Performance* (New York: Columbia University Press, 1941).

[4] Stephen Farnum and John Watkins, *The Watkins-Farnum Performance Scale* (Winona, Minn.: Hal Leonard Music, Inc., 1954; String Edition, 1969).

represents the scoring attempts of many teachers trying to follow directions that are clear but complicated. The Watkins-Farnum scale is described in greater detail in Chapter Eight.

An area of evaluation that has produced several important tests is that of auditory-visual skills. These are the skills that enable one to hear what he sees on the musical page or to visualize the note symbols for music he is hearing. Auditory-visual skills are akin to sight-reading skills, but not identical. The instrumental sight-reader can use the written notes as signals to put certain fingers down, so that he sight-reads pitch very successfully without the necessity for hearing the notes mentally. The act of rhythm reading is nearer to auditory-visual skill, for accurate rendition of rhythm symbols depends upon hearing them inwardly. The sight singer who depends upon relative pitch and knowledge of intervals uses a skill also closely akin to auditory-visual discrimination. Auditory-visual discrimination is one of the most important skills for a musician to possess, because it gives him access to music without waiting for it to be performed. The conductor studying a score, the teacher selecting new music for students, the child thumbing through a songbook, to say nothing of the composer and the arranger, use auditory-visual skills. These skills have a positive correlation with sight-reading skills but do not depend upon a motor skill for their demonstration; even if the individual cannot play well enough to execute a four-measure phrase properly, he may be able to demonstrate that he understands the musical symbols that portray the phrase.

One of the most elementary hearing skills is the ability to recognize tonal center, to understand what *1* or *do* means, and to locate by ear the pitch *do* for many different melodies in many different keys. A method for testing as well as for practicing this skill is to have students listen to music, then select the tonal center from several choices played for them. Other aural skills include recognition of mode, meter, intervals, cadences, rhythm patterns, harmony, and others. The teacher can select or create short musical items to which students must listen for one or more of the features mentioned above. Evaluation can follow exactly the same method: students listen to brief selections and identify orally or by multiple-choice the meter, mode, or whatever. The *Music Achievement Tests* (MAT)[5] include sections measuring a number of these skills. The Gaston tests[6] also offer measurement for some aural skills.

---

[5] Richard Colwell, *Music Achievement Tests* (Chicago: Follett Educational Corporation, 1968–69–70).

[6] E. Thayer Gaston, *A Test of Musicality*, 4th ed., revised (Lawrence, Kan.: Odell's Instrumental Service, 1957).

Measures that test auditory-visual skill combine listening and reading. The Farnum test[7] and the Knuth test[8] have sections on combined pitch and rhythm. MAT has separate sections for pitch and rhythm, as do the Aliferis college entrance and midpoint tests.[9, 10]

Reading skills are sometimes differentiated from both sight-reading and auditory-visual skills. They are then meant to designate the individual's ability to play or sing music not at sight but after he has had a chance to study the music. The focus is on the accuracy with which the performer reads music he has rehearsed. The teacher can test this skill individually by assigning any appropriate music to the student to read at a designated time. The testing situation can be made more realistic by requiring the student to perform his music against an accompanying bass line, while all the other parts are being played, against a contrapuntal melody, or against an independent rhythmic line. Depending upon the music, the added feature may make reading easier or more difficult; in evaluating, the teacher must be able to discern which.

The more active version of auditory-visual skills is the ability to write down what is heard. This skill is emphasized in all college freshman theory courses much to the distress of those students lacking in such skills. Musical dictation requires the listener to write down accurately the symbols for what is being played: melodic line, rhythm, harmony, or some combination of these. The skill used in taking musical dictation is very serviceable for the teacher and the composer-arranger. Professional performers may never need it after they leave the freshman or sophomore level in college, but the musician whose work requires a creative element can make good use of this skill. Dictation can be evaluated by group measure, just as it is taught. The teacher may use an instrument or voice to present the pattern for dictation; these may range in difficulty from a two-note interval to a complete phrase or a brief three-part form. Dictation skill, although it is easy to measure, is difficult to teach and to learn.

Rhythmic skill has been referred to several times and may be evaluated in a number of ways depending upon what type of rhythmic skill is in question. Recognition of pulse, tempo, and meter are perhaps the

---

[7] Stephen Farnum, *Farnum Music Test* (Riverside, R.I.: Bond Publishing Co., 1969).

[8] William Knuth, *Achievement Tests in Music* (Monmouth, Ore.: Creative Arts Research Associates, 1967).

[9] James Aliferis, *Aliferis Music Achievement Test* (Minneapolis: University of Minnesota Press, 1954). Distributed by Harcourt, Brace & World, Inc.

[10] James Aliferis and John Stecklein, *Aliferis-Stecklein Music Achievement Test* (Minneapolis: University of Minnesota Press, 1962). Distributed by Harcourt, Brace & World, Inc.

basic responses to rhythm; these can be evaluated by having students move in some specified manner to music they hear. At more advanced levels, students may be asked to perform a pattern given them aurally, a written pattern, or a pattern indicated by its name, such as two against three. Sight-reading tests, reading tests, auditory-visual tests, and dictation tests all can be used solely for measuring rhythmic understanding and recognition. Any test of performance in this area can be taped for later listening by the evaluator, since rhythm is much less tangible than pitch and may necessitate closer listening for an accurate evaluation.

INSTRUMENTAL SKILL TOOLS

Instrumental skills are those skills that control the instrument, giving the player mastery over it. These include embouchure formation, knowledge of fingering and finger facility, breathing, tonguing, bowing, and other acts related to the instrument itself. These may be measured only by individual scrutiny. Whole treatises of medical-type analysis have been written on how these skills are accomplished. X-ray pictures have been taken of the physical mechanism at work in embouchure, diaphragm, etc.; light probes have been constructed and placed in the throat to determine glottal action and other aspects of formant production for the vocalist. Information from these analytical writings can be of help in instruction and evaluation. A careful analysis of tonguing, such as that by Edlefsen[11] can increase the teacher's perception of problems. The use of the tongue and the throat can only be judged by the sounds produced, but the teacher can by demonstration and explanation help the player form good habits or correct bad ones. With external production of sound such as that of the string, percussion, or keyboard instruments, photographs and moving films can reveal much about use of the fingers, hands, arms, and entire body. Clarinet-playing techniques have been evaluated cinefluorographically by Anfinson.[12] The detailed pictorial analysis of violin playing done by Hodgson[13] is a good illustration of this tool's usefulness in evaluation and learning. Reimer discovered a unique means for evaluating snare drum rudiments. A piece of carbon paper is inserted between two sheets of bond paper and placed on a responsive surface.

---

[11] Blaine Edlefsen, "Symbolization and Articulation of Oboe Tones" (Doctoral dissertation, Eastman School of Music, 1966).

[12] Roland Anfinson, "A Cinefluorographic Investigation of Selected Clarinet Playing Techniques" (Doctoral dissertation, State University of Iowa, 1965).

[13] Percival Hodgson, *Motion Study and Violin Bowing* (Urbana, Ill.: American String Teachers Association, 1958).

A small circle is drawn on the top sheet of paper to correspond with the area on the drum where the rudiments should be played. After the player has executed a rudiment on the paper-covered surface, the strength, grouping and number can be determined by the carbon marks on the second sheet of paper. A similar device using either carbon paper or electronic impulses can be devised to measure evenness of touch on the piano. Prepared pianos with various lighting panels or other means of recording can tell the player what notes were played incorrectly in scales, chords, harmonizations, or compositions, depending upon how the evaluative device is programed. Many of these things are impractical for the average teacher; they are found in research laboratories or in school systems where finances are available for expensive tools. Nevertheless, it is well to be informed about the possibilities for electronic or computer type aid in learning. Such equipment will become more and more common as more uses are found for it.

Vocal Skill Tools

Tone production can be evaluated visually by the use of an FM discriminator, which shows the vibration picture of a performer's tone for him to match against a picture of a model tone. Jack Heller of the University of Connecticut has experimented with using this device for perception and learning. He has studied both tone production and pitch accuracy. The performer learns by adjusting his pitch or his loudness until it matches the model pitch/tone shown on the discriminator. In this manner he is evaluating himself against an objective model and at the same time learning what the *feel* is for acceptable pitch and tone production.

Research Devices

A factor in music reading is eye motion. The movement of the eyes helps determine the speed of the reading, though not the accuracy. Considerable research has been invested in the use of tachistoscopes to improve music reading. This instrument flashes a small portion of music on the screen at a set speed, and the learner attempts to read as much as possible in the time the musical fragment is shown. Speed can be reduced or increased according to the needs of the learner. Other optical devices can determine whether the eye is reading ahead, perceiving patterns, or moving note by note. These latter devices can also be used to determine the speed of reading and whether entire phrases are grasped, as well as the actual pattern of eye movement. Such machines cannot evaluate music reading, of course, but may be helpful in determining the reasons for poor reading.

Considering all of the methods and tools described above for evaluating musical skills, decisions need to be made as to which of these are appropriate for any situation. Standards need to be set for all skills; weaknesses and strengths need to be determined and areas of emphasis selected. The instructor must bear the greatest share of responsibility for these actions, but students can be given practice in thinking about skill goals and evaluation by listing potential objectives and suggesting standards they think appropriate. The teacher may solicit the opinions of nonmusicians as well. Administrators who make decisions concerning the music program might develop more insight and sympathy if they give some thought to the variety of skills and the diversity of levels present in music.

QUESTIONS FOR DISCUSSION

1. List several evaluative tools that do not measure the actual skill but measure an item closely correlated with the skill.
2. What skill levels seem to be appropriate learning experiences for first-grade children?
3. Construct checklists or rating scales for several skills commonly taught at the high school level.
4. Evaluate the adequacy of the rating form used in your state music contest.
5. When evaluating a skill, must the evaluation be restricted to technique, or can skills be taught and evaluated according to high musical standards?
6. What motor skills appear to be reversible for the purpose of evaluation?
7. What methods of evaluation are currently in use to appraise the effects of drill?
8. Construct some additional skills check sheets that provide definitive statements on the level of development expected.
9. Develop a variety of descriptive words usable in identifying levels of skill development in your field.
10. Discuss the most important psychomotor objectives for each level of the taxonomy in music education. See Appendix A.
11. Identify different methods of evaluation and create sample questions for each level of the taxonomy.

REFERENCES

Berg, Harry ed., *Evaluation in Social Studies,* Thirty-fifth Yearbook of the National Council for the Social Studies. Washington, D.C.: National Council for the Social Studies, 1965, Chapter 5.

Simpson, Elizabeth, *The Classification of Educational Objectives, Psychomotor Domain.* Washington, D.C.: USOE final report OE 5-85-104, 1966.

Whybrew, William, *Measurement and Evaluation in Music.* Dubuque, Iowa: Wm. C. Brown Company, Publishers, 1962, Chapter 11.

CHAPTER SEVEN

evaluating the affective domain

DEFINING THE AFFECTIVE DOMAIN

The cognitive and psychomotor domains deal with items and actions that are overt, can be seen and recognized. The affective domain, on the other hand, is almost entirely covert and internal and must be inferred from acts, verbal statements, tone of voice, facial expressions, and similar inexact clues. Obviously, there is a large area of human experience not covered by knowledge and skill, an area in which learning takes place and that is considered within the purview of the educational system. It is difficult to define this area clearly enough to help in teaching and learning since it falls neither into the neat patterns of skill development nor into the hierarchy of cognitive learning. The affective domain is concerned with emotions and feelings, with sensitivity and awareness. However, these terms are of no help in planning educational experiences; and so must be translated into words that indicate a visible sign of the affect. Those who discuss teaching and measuring the affective domain use such categories as opinion, belief, response, attitude, interest, appreciation, empathy, and value. There is much overlapping among the categories and only fine shades of difference between them. The importance of these terms for music education is not so much whether they can form a neat and logical taxonomy, but whether they can be helpful as guides in teaching and evaluation.

Current literature in music education, including this book, emphasizes the importance of aesthetic response. Writers and thinkers in the field are in general agreement that the unique contribution that music can make is in fostering the aesthetic sensitivity of the young person; indeed, aesthetic education is seen as the prime purpose for including the arts in the public school schedule. The term *aesthetic response* is noticeably absent from the preceding definition of the affective domain. None of the other categories—attitude, appreciation, even value—has the same meaning or connotes the same kind of experience as aesthetic response. Omission of aesthetic response from the categories of the affective domain does not indicate that it is unimportant, but only that it applies to a specialized area of education. Conceivably, one can have an aesthetic response to any area of learning—statements are occasionally made about the tremendous aesthetic response a mathematician has to a beautifully worked out equation—but we are on firmer ground if we seek to apply our thinking only to the area of the fine arts. The elements of cognition and psychomotor are present in the aesthetic experience, but the basic essential is, perhaps, value.

TEACHING FOR AFFECTIVE RESPONSE

The school is established to transmit information, but also to teach values. Belief in learning and in the right of each individual to have opportunity to learn is a value rather than a fact. The problem the school has in transmitting values along with facts stems from its practice of the democratic principle. In a free society, each individual should be allowed to choose his own beliefs and work out his own attitudes. The school neither can nor wishes to force him into a conforming pattern. The student is free to like what he wishes, honor what he wishes, appreciate what he deems worthy, and ignore what he deems unworthy, as long as he does not violate the rules that guard the same rights for others. The teachers and administrators of the school may be distressed by his choices, but they cannot, and usually will not, attempt to alter them beyond the gentle means of example and persuasion. The problem remains: Should the school try to indoctrinate, or should it assume near neutrality? The first course may destroy initiative and freedom of creative thought, but the latter course may result in the loss of the beliefs upon which the society rests. A man's attitudes and values are his personal affair and should not be structured by educational institutions. However, if everyone is left to make his own choices as to what is better and poorer, man remains rather primitive and crude; the elements of civilization are not to be rediscovered by every generation, but are to be passed on, saving the best while discarding the mediocre and outmoded.

The solution of this dilemma seems to be to keep evaluation of the affective domain separate from the giving of grades. The grade is the reward or penalty for the student's efforts in school. This may be unsatisfactory, but it is a fact. If the development of attitudes and values is to be free from authoritarianism, it must never be mixed with decisions concerning academic grades. The grade stands for achievement in skill or knowledge or both, but never has and should not represent the total growth of the student. Many areas besides the affective lie outside the grading system: social growth, psychological adjustment, emotional development. Although the school is concerned about these and recognizes changes in these areas, they are not reflected in the grades received. The fact that no grade is given for affective development does not do away with the need for evaluating this important area. The teacher needs to know what attitudes are being formed in order to know how to proceed further in the affective domain, but as in all evaluation, the principal use of the knowledge is for improvement of instruction. The music teacher has a major task; he needs to recognize what values should be emphasized and presented to students, and he needs to measure the reactions of students in order to know whether these values are indeed being communicated successfully.

As with all areas of teaching and learning, the objectives for affective growth must be stated in behavioral terms. This is considerably more difficult than for cognition or skills where the desired outcomes can be evaluated through actions, statements, paper and pencil tests, and required tasks. Nevertheless, sufficient research has been done in measuring the affective domain that teachers who will word their objectives carefully can determine whether or not progress is being made toward them. An objective such as "seeks out and prefers the better music," could be restated to "attends concerts of classical and semiclassical music; selects T.V. and radio programs of classical and semiclassical music in preference to pop or commercial music" [the author is not suggesting objectives; it could be "selects pop music in preference to other kinds," if that conforms to the teacher's objective]; "recognizes and enjoys music characterized by good tone quality, skillful execution, appropriate instrumentation, and genuineness of communication whether it is jazz, folk, entertainment, or any other kind of music." When a statement takes this form, the teacher can devise situations in which the student makes choices between different kinds of music or different kinds of events to test for achievement of the objective. It is clear that objectives such as developing a love of great music, imparting an awareness of the cultural heritage, or growth of skills and knowledge for appreciating great music are of minimal use in planning and conducting learning experiences. What is great music? How can love be recognized? What are the signs of awareness? Which skills and knowledge are the appropriate ones for appreciation? The affective domain need not remain cloudy and vague where curriculum planners, philosophers, and teachers are willing to wrestle with clear definitions of the acts and attitudes involved in desirable responses to music.

The Formation of Attitudes and Values

Some skepticism exists as to whether the public school can make any significant changes in the affective development of the individual. The school day is relatively brief and represents an artificial situation; how can it then hope to have any influence upon the habits of reacting and the emotional patterns built up in the preschool years and the *real* contacts outside the school hours? Studies in this area have had inconclusive and contradictory results. At least one piece of research, by Sanford at Vassar,[1] concluded that basic attitudes, opinions, and values can be changed over the four-year college experience, while another study of beliefs[2] came to the opposite conclusion. At any rate, there are not enough negative findings to furnish an excuse for the avoidance of affective learnings in music. Whether teaching for values actually alters the basic viewpoint of the student or only brings into consciousness emotions and reactions that were latent or unobserved, the teacher has an obligation to help the student experience the aesthetic satisfactions of music and understand how these are arrived at.

In practical experience, a person rarely develops an instinctive appreciation for music without knowing anything about it. Cognitive awareness heightens the emotional response, sharpens the attention, and helps to create a genuine aesthetic experience. Many psychologists believe the affective and cognitive domains to be closely related and interrelated. Rokeach states:

> We assume that every affective state also has its representation
> as a cognitive state in the form of some belief or some struc-
> tural relation among beliefs within a system. With respect to
> the enjoyment of music, for example, we all build up through
> past experience a set of beliefs or expectancies about what con-
> stitutes *good* or *bad* music. It is in terms of such expectancies,

---

[1] Harry Berg, ed., *Evaluation in Social Studies,* Thirty-fifth Yearbook of the National Council for the Social Studies (Washington, D.C.: NCSS, 1965), p. 125. Quoted in an article "Measurement of Noncognitive Objectives in the Social Studies" by Lewis Mayhew.

[2] *Ibid.,* p. 124.

which are more often implicit than explicit, that we enjoy a particular composition.[3]

In any learning situation involving musical response, an overlapping of the cognitive and the affective is necessitated by the demands of verbalization; to put into words something about music means thinking about it, using terms accurately and with understanding. One's very expectations about how the music is going to sound are based upon some intellectual learning; we remember the sound of an orchestra or a jazz combo, we know the meaning of *march* or *minuet,* we mentally seek for a melody or a meter to give the sounds organization, and so forth.

The fact that cognition is a legitimate part of the affective response to music helps simplify the problems of measuring affective response. Evaluation of attitudes and values, though intricate, is possible because many aspects can be verbalized, put into specific statements, and clearly pointed out by teacher or student. The responsibility of the school program is then to teach the substance upon which understanding is based and to expect students to form their own values and to experience the aesthetic response as a result of what they know and what they hear in the music. The task of the school is to give students sufficient information and understanding to make their own intelligent decisions. The music program must, therefore, offer a cosmopolitan sampling of many kinds of music, with a clear communication of the basis, origin, and significance of each. Evidence exists that emotional reaction cannot be taught in any genuine sense; a teacher may lead the student to know what he is supposed to feel, but he cannot teach him to have that feeling. The music program can set the stage carefully and provide models, but whether the inner drama takes place, and its exact pattern, will depend upon each individual.

EVALUATING THE AFFECTIVE DOMAIN

PROBLEMS OF MEASUREMENT

Three major problems deserve attention here. The first problem is that most measurement uses words—asking questions, eliciting responses to various kinds of statements, requiring that choices be made—and the student who discovers what sort of thing is being measured may make the responses he considers appropriate, whether true or not. His words may not match his actions. Often the student may feel he is answering

---

[3] Milton Rokeach, *The Open and Closed Mind* (New York: Basic Books, Inc., 1960), p. 399.

honestly but would be contradicted by his own actions; or the desire to conform may lead the student to make dishonest answers. The widely known study by Corey,[4] in which students whose attitudes condemned cheating continued to cheat, is the classic example of this. A second problem is that evaluation may not be able to differentiate between value responses that come as a result of maturity and those that are the consequence of education. The concerns of society that are satisfied by merely living in society for twenty years should be recognized, so that the school does not fritter away its resources upon goals that are achieved naturally. In the affective domain, this latter type of goal might include the pleasure-emotive reaction to music and responses to conspicuous rhythmic, dynamic, and color effects. Television and film drama are permeated with music that elicits the pleasure-emotive reaction, so that maturation in our society pretty well ensures opportunity for growth of this response. The third problem is with the creation of the measurement device. Most evaluative tools for the affective domain consist of a series of statements to which the student reacts, or of multiple-choice items in which each answer represents a somewhat different value. Such statements must not be obvious, they must all be worded to sound *good,* and the choices must be such that most will appear to be equally desirable. Construction of such an instrument is difficult and requires thought as to exactly what each response might indicate. In addition, the answers are harder to interpret than for cognition questions, for they may contradict each other or exhibit inconsistencies. Because of the complex nature of attitudes and values, most persons hold some views that conflict with others and display acts that cannot be reconciled with other acts. The measurement tools that have been most successful for the affective domain have been worked out by carefully checking an individual's answers with his actions, by comparing responses to each question with the total score to discover which questions showed inconsistencies. A short description of the best of these tools can help to illustrate how a device might be constructed for music.

Value Scales and Measurements

The first systematic attempt to measure attitude was done in 1929 by Thurstone.[5] He collected several hundred statements from people reflecting how each one felt about the subject. The statements were then

---

4 Berg, *Evaluation in Social Studies,* p. 117.

5 L. L. Thurstone, *The Measurement of Values* (Chicago: The University of Chicago Press, 1959). First reprinted in L. L. Thurstone and E. J. Chase, *The Measurement of Attitudes* (Chicago: The University of Chicago Press, 1929).

sorted by experts until agreement was reached as to the position each statement reflected. For each area to be explored, eleven or twenty-one statements were selected, each statement having a numerical value that indicated how strongly it reflected a positive or negative view towards the area in question. The person taking the test simply checked the statements with which he agreed, and his score was computed by adding the numerical values of those statements. The statements were in random order, and the answerer had no knowledge of the weight given each statement. The Thurstone scales seemed consistent but were very time-consuming and expensive to construct.

The Likert scale[6] also uses a series of attitude statements, but rather than weighting the statements, a five-choice answer is used: *strongly approve, approve, undecided, disapprove, and strongly disapprove.* These responses are scored ranging from 5 for *strongly approve* to 1 for *strongly disapprove,* all of the statements being positive.

The Allport-Vernon system[7] uses the technique of forced choice. The answerer is forced to select between two statements, both of which might seem equally sound or desirable; for example, in music a choice might be required between the works of two equally great composers. The test has been criticized because of the forced scale but can be defended on the basis that choices become important only when a conflict exists between two relatively equal possibilities.

As research in this area accumulated, techniques became somewhat more sophisticated. The armed forces during World War II developed tests in which situations were described and the individual was asked to check statements illustrating his reaction to the situation. Inferences would then be drawn from the pattern or characteristics revealed by the total set of answers.

Projective devices are those in which the individual is given some sort of ambiguous situation, such as a statement or picture, and is asked to explain the situation as he interprets it. He then projects his own biases and emotions as he explains what the picture or statement means to him. A second kind of projective device makes use of open-ended sentences, which the individual must complete. For music, items might be: (1) Symphony orchestras should be _____. (2) Most of the music on radio and television is _____. (3) If all of the works of Beethoven were lost, _____. Construction of such items is relatively easy, but it is obviously impossible to interpret the answers in any

---

[6] R. A. Likert, "A Technique for the Measurement of Attitudes," *Archives Psychology,* No. 140 (1932).

[7] G. W. Allport, P. E. Vernon, and G. Lindzey, *Study of Values,* 3rd ed. (Boston: Houghton Mifflin Company, 1960).

numerical or objective fashion. Projective devices have been found to be unreliable, as well as to elicit contradictory answers from the same individual. Nevertheless, they can offer some clues in a general way and may be helpful in situations where other types of evaluation seem less accessible.

The classic evaluative tool for affect in music is the work of Kate Hevner (Mueller)[8] in 1934. The test consists of forty-eight short excerpts from the beginning phrases of piano compositions, each paired with a mutilated version in which one element of the piece—rhythm, melody, or harmony—has been altered. Subjects respond by indicating which version is the better and the element that has been altered in the poorer one. The test was found to be low in reliability and validity below the college level. It does not measure musicality because the alteration of the music in essence makes it a different piece of music, and the choice becomes one of preference. However, if changing the preferences of students towards the more familiar or normal sound in music is an objective, this tool is a valid one. The use of semiclassical piano music quickly dated some of the items; Newell Long, supported by the U.S. Office of Education, revised the test in 1965.[9] The newer version includes string quartet, woodwind quintet, and organ music in addition to piano music, has a widened repertoire making use of more Baroque and contemporary items, and includes items in which the two versions in each question are identical. The test was standardized in 1967 using a nonrandom sample of about 4,400 students. Reliability of the test is .383 for fifth-grade students, .444 for junior high school students, .571 for college students, and .607 for graduate music students. Long's research is currently the only project of any size in the affective area. In 1969–70 he conducted a pilot study to develop the *Music Discrimination Test* for younger students, using shorter items in a simpler context to measure understanding of concepts such as rhythm, melody, and harmony, to apply these to musical listening, and to measure judgment of musical value.

A slightly different but related test is one constructed by Schoen, *Tests of Musical Feeling and Understanding*,[10] in which test items contain phrases that are identical except for the ending, and the listener is to choose which phrase has the most appropriate ending. For each item,

[8] Kate Hevner, "Appreciation of Music and Tests for the Appreciation of Music," *Studies in Appreciation of Art* (University of Oregon Publication), IV, 6 (1934), 83–151.

[9] Newell Long, "A Revision of the University of Oregon Music Discrimination Test" (Doctoral dissertation, Indiana University, 1965).

[10] Max Schoen, "Tests of Musical Feeling and Musical Understanding," *Journal of Comparative Psychology*, V (1925), pp. 31–52.

the listener checks the most appropriate description from the following: *balance created, belonging, togetherness, unity, variety,* and *finality.*

One of the most thorough jobs of test construction in terms of summarizing research in the affective domain is found in Kyme's doctoral dissertation entitled "The Value of Aesthetic Judgments in the Assessment of Musical Capacity."[11] Kyme's battery includes both preference items and items that require some knowledge to select the appropriate response. The short version of his test was derived as part of the thesis and remains unpublished; nine tests of the preliminary battery are most appropriate for discussion here.

1. Instrumental solos were selected from performances at music festivals and from commercial recordings. Judgments were to be made on the appropriateness of intonation, tone quality, phrasing, interpretation, tempo, rhythm, and dynamics performed by string and woodwind performers.

2. Vocal and instrumental chamber music introduced the factors of balance, diction and blend to be used in determining the better of two performances.

3. and 4. Orchestra performances by both professional and school orchestras and symphonic band were used. Answers refer to tone quality, rhythm, balance, and so on.

5. Piano items, including popular music, employed the mutilated technique on one of the paired items. Harmony, melody, or rhythm was changed In some examples, the change was rather subtle, employing such devices as modulating without the proper preparation or simple versus full harmonic accompaniment.

6. Two harmonized versions of a Bartók melody were to be compared in determining intervals. Choices included selecting the harmonization using consecutive diatonic thirds or the one employing consecutive diatonic sixths or the version using tempered or justly tuned bars.

7. This test presented ten paired cadences to be judged according to their sense of finality.

8. Here, folksongs were used with changes in chord patterns of the Autoharp accompaniment, the changes ranging from slight to relatively drastic ones. One example used the same harmony but two tempi, and in another the style, defined as brilliance and enthusiasm, was destroyed in the poorer version.

9. This test required the student to listen to ten selections and select the best descriptive adjective. For example, Mendelssohn's "Scherzo"

---

11 George Kyme, "The Value of Aesthetic Judgments in the Assessment of Musical Capacity" (Doctoral dissertation, University of California, 1954).

was described as mischievous, exciting, or happy, with mischievous the keyed answer.

The reliability of the Kyme tests is reported to be above .70, with apparently acceptable validity as based upon correlations with the rankings of high school musicians by their directors and others. The given validity coefficient of .74 is probably spuriously high, but many of the ideas advanced by Kyme warrant further serious investigation.

A number of preference tests have been devised in which the student makes choices among different compositions or musical items. The Keston preference test contains thirty questions; in each question, the listener chooses which one of four compositions he prefers. As an example, the recorded excerpts for one question are the Mendelssohn "Scherzo" from *A Midsummer Night's Dream,* the Chabrier "Spanish Rhapsody," Morton Gould's "Adios Muchachos," and Tommy Dorsey's "Song of India." A similar but much older test is the Trabue *Scales for Measuring Judgment of Orchestral Music* (1920),[12] which uses sixteen orchestral compositions presented in groups of three or four. The *Kwalwasser Tests of Melodic Sensitivity and Harmonic Sensitivity*[13] ask the listener to choose the better of two short examples paired on differences in either melody or harmony. A 1910 test for interval preference by Valentine,[14] now outdated, found the greatest preference to be for the major third, minor third next, then octave, ranging down to the minor second.

Several researchers have been interested in the communication of mood in music. Schoen and Gatewood[15] obtained data on some 20,000 responses to vocal and instrumental phonograph records, concluding that musical compositions did produce a mood change.

An adjective circle devised by Hevner and revised by Farnsworth[16] has a high reliability. The circle consists of ten categories of mood terms, each category just slightly different from the category on either side, in the manner of a color wheel. The student listens to a composition and selects the category in which he finds a word describing the mood of the

---

[12] M. R. Trabue, "Scales for Measuring Judgment of Orchestral Music," *Journal of Educational Psychology,* XIV (1923), pp. 545–561.

[13] J. Kwalwasser, *Tests of Melodic and Harmonic Sensitivity* (Camden, N.J.: Victor Talking Machine Co., 1926).

[14] C. W. Valentine, "The Aesthetic Appreciation of Musical Intervals Among School Children and Adults," *British Journal of Psychology,* VI (1913), p. 190; VII (1914), p. 108.

[15] Robert W. Lundin, *An Objective Psychology of Music,* 2nd ed. (New York: The Ronald Press Company, 1967), p. 160.

[16] P. R. Farnsworth, "A Study of the Hevner Adjective List," *Journal of Aesthetics and Art Criticism,* XIII (1954), pp. 97–103.

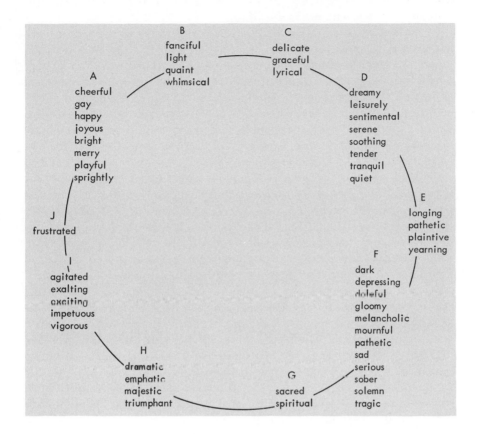

music for him. Careful selection of music brought about highly homogeneous results.

An early music appreciation test is that by Fisher,[17] in which the student listens and chooses the correct response from four choices for mood, association and imagery, or rhythmic response. Mood studies also include tests by Hevner[18] and Heinlein[19] to determine the affect of major and minor modes upon the listener. They concluded that minor mode and major mode communicated distinguishably different moods

17 W. R. Fisher, "The Construction and Validation of an Instrument to Measure Musical Appreciation" (Doctoral dissertation, Boston University, 1949).

18 K. Hevner, "The Affective Character of Major and Minor Modes in Music," *American Journal of Psychology*, XLVII (1935), pp. 103–118.

19 C. Heinlein, "The Affective Characters of Major and Minor Modes in Music," *Journal of Comparative Psychology*, VIII (1928), pp. 101–142.

but that tempo, pitch, range, and timbre also seemed to be factors, especially for subjects with musical training.

Paper and pencil tests to measure attitude have focused upon various aspects of music and music training. These include ranking composers in order of importance; responding to statements about high school music experience or about musical activities generally; responding to statements concerning the characteristics of music teachers or music education practices. Other paper and pencil tests ask the student to examine hypothetical concert programs and rank them, require elementary teachers to rank their own adequacy on various musical skills, or test elementary students' attitudes towards music.

Two tests in the affective domain fail to fit into any of the above categories, and are of sufficient interest to merit a short description here. A musical concepts test constructed by Hevner in 1957 consists of a short composition that is heard three times.[20] After each hearing, the student answers descriptive statements about the piece using a five-point scale from *strongly agree* to *strongly disagree*. The same statements are used for each hearing, and answers are compared to show changes as the piece becomes more familiar. The second test, by Crickmore,[21] is for the assessment of musical experience. It consists of a simple answer scale using terms such as *interested, desire to talk, more relaxed, no change, happier,* and so forth. The listener responds after he has heard a musical selection, specifying any change that the music made in his emotional state.

Omitted from the preceding paragraphs has been any mention of studies in physiological response to music. Although testing of physiological response is beyond the domain of the music teacher, research in this area is interesting and significant. The first objective measurement in music came from psychologists who, at the turn of the twentieth century, studied the effect of music upon physiological functions. Their findings, corroborated many times, were that the body is actively involved in musical listening. Breathing, cardiac activity, blood supply, and cell membranes all show changes as a result of musical listening. As Lundin puts it, "The entire response equipment of the organism is directed wholeheartedly toward the stimulus object."[22] Training appears to be a factor, for differences in physical reaction to various kinds of music were found to exist between trained and untrained subjects.

20 Hevner, *op. cit.*

21 L. Crickmore, "An Approach to the Measurement of Music Appreciation," *Journal of Research in Music Education,* XXVI, 3 (1968), pp. 239–253.

22 Lundin, *An Objective Psychology of Music,* p. 199.

TEACHER-CONSTRUCTED MEASURES

Rating Scales

The teacher can derive numerous ideas for affective measures from the preceding description of tests. Utilization of these ideas takes care and skill, however, if the true feelings and values of students are to be discovered. A *rating scale* appears to be simple to construct, involving only the selection of items to be put in order of value by the student. Oppenheim[23] says that the use of ratings invites the gravest dangers and possible errors, that in the hands of untutored persons the rating scale is useless. The real danger seems to be that it has a spurious air of accuracy upon which undue reliance may be placed. When used in conjunction with a variety of other evaluative devices, rating scales can help discover how students feel about the school music activities, about specific kinds of music, about the teacher, and about out-of-school music participation.

Attitude Scales and Projective Tests

Attitude scales and *projective tests* can also be constructed by the teacher, but these are more difficult than the rating scale. The way in which statements are worded can imply what the correct answer should be. The wording of a statement may be so vague that an answer to it gives no useful information. Each statement in an attitude scale should be pointed toward a single, specific attitude or value, and should ask for a multiple-choice response such as those described earlier—*strongly agree, agree, no opinion, disagree,* and *strongly disagree,* or a similar set. Attitude statements should be tried out on colleagues or on a group other than that for which the measure is intended, to reveal discrepancies, omissions, ambiguities, and obvious wording. The measure can then be revised to be more effective. For example, a question such as, "Our unit on jazz has changed my ideas about African music: *strongly agree, agree, no opinion, disagree, strongly disagree,*" tells the teacher little. Rewording it to read, "The jazz rhythms and melodic improvisation coming from African music are: (a) exciting and important, (b) good for entertainment but not for serious music, (c) all right for others to listen to but I

---

[23] A. N. Oppenheim, *Questionnaire Design and Attitude Measurement* (New York: Basic Books, Inc., 1966), p. 84.

don't care for them, (d) ugly and meaningless," can yield more information.

A preference scale is a type of interest inventory used to indicate preferences for types of music, activities in the classroom, or other aspects where liking is an important objective. If the teacher is focusing upon developing a liking for music and music class, some systematic method of measuring this is essential. One method is to have the students rank their school subjects, rank their ten favorite activities, rank their ten favorite musical selections, and so on. They may rank items from a list given to them or make their own list, as the teacher desires. In order to get honest answers, the purpose of the scale must be disguised; it should be administered during homeroom period, a study period, or some similar period. The school guidance counselor can administer the scale, thus making it unrelated to a specific teacher or class.

Attitude scales differ from preference scales in that they are designed to measure negative as well as positive feelings and the individual is not forced to make first choice, second choice, and so on. Often, students take the easy way out and circle responses at random without differentiating between *like a little* and *it's OK,* or whatever the choices might be. Therefore, an alternative technique has been devised in which grouping is permitted but the grouping is forced into a range that allows for discrimination. Usually, some variation of the normal distribution is sought. The teacher needs to decide how many categories are desirable. When this is done, the procedure is as follows. If knowledge is sought concerning attitudes toward twenty musical selections, the teacher might decide to divide the preferences into five categories: *most favorite, favorite, all right, disliked,* and *most disliked.* He would ask students to put the titles into five piles, one in the *most favorite* category, three in the *favorite* pile, twelve in the *all right* pile, three in the *disliked* pile, and one in the *most disliked* pile. To make the selecting easier for the student, he may be told to divide the twenty into two equal piles of *like* and *dislike,* and to divide each of these into two equal piles of greater and lesser preference. Then he has only to select the *most favorite* from the top pile and the *most disliked* from the bottom pile, and move one more selection from the top pile down into the middle one, from the bottom pile up into the middle one. He has then arrived at the numerical distribution asked for, 1, 3, 12, 3, 1. This is called a *Q sort technique;* more complete descriptions may be found in measurement textbooks. Any number of groups and any gradation may be used, so long as the extreme high and low preferences are one in number and the groups graduate in size toward the middle choice, which is the largest group. If such gradation is too complicated for the teacher's purpose, selections may be put into equal groups. This type of forced preference is helpful though not as accurate, for it does not require critical thinking from the student in determining the best and the worst of the choices. The teacher who does not wish to force anything into a *dislike* category is misguided. Henry Dyer says, "The only kind of test situation which can contribute to the measurement process is one that evokes differing responses from the individuals whose behavior is being measured."[24] When students are allowed to say they like everything, the teacher finds out nothing about preference, discrimination, or attitude.

QUESTIONNAIRES, CHECKLISTS, AND OTHER DEVICES

Other types of measures that the teacher can construct include the following. The *questionnaire* is a type of attitude scale made much use of in opinion polls and research studies. The basic difference between a questionnaire and an attitude scale is that the response choices in a questionnaire usually have a wider range, taking any form desired by the question writer.

Value tests can make use of recorded musical items in a manner similar to tests described in the previous section: different performances of the same music can be compared; altered versions can be compared with the original; a multiple-choice value answer can be checked for each work or excerpt heard; choices can be made between good and bad chord progressions, good and bad cadences for the same phrases, good and bad tone quality, and so on.

A written device containing *activity choices* can be helpful. It will not yield a measurable, quantitative score but will help to indicate general attitude. Questions can be constructed such as, "When you have an unexpected hour of free time, which of these would you be most likely to do: read, watch TV, listen to popular recordings, go outside to play, practice, work at an inside hobby," or, "If you were given a present of $15 and told to spend it any way you pleased, which of these would you be most likely to buy: clothes, game equipment such as tennis racket or ice skates, classical recordings, hobby equipment such as a model kit or paints, books, none of these."

The *checklist* also applies to the affective area. For example, "Check all of the terms you feel apply to you: healthy, cheerful, selfish, musical, dumb, generous, good-looking, introvert, artistic, intelligent, dishonest," or, "Check all of the terms which apply to (1) your pres-

---

[24] Henry Dyer, "Educational Measurement: Its Nature and Its Problems," *Evaluation in Social Studies,* Thirty-fifth Yearbook of the National Council for the Social Studies (Washington, D.C.: NCSS, 1965), p. 23.

ent English class, (2) your present music class, (3) your present mathematics class: I have learned a lot; I hate it; the subject interests me; the teacher makes it boring; I can't see any use for it; we never learn anything new; it's my favorite subject."

Students can take stock of themselves on *personal inventories.* These checklists can be used with younger children as well as with those who are more mature. Questions that smaller children might ask themselves would include, "Do I pay attention in class?" "How long can I listen to music before I begin to think about something else?" "Can I clap in time to the music?" "How many key signatures do I recognize?" "How many instruments of the orchestra do I know when I see them? when I hear them?" and so forth.

Daily logs kept over a short period or a *critical incident test* are useful. The former asks the student to keep a record for a week or two weeks of every musical activity he experiences: listening to music on the radio, attending choir rehearsal, listening to a friend's record, practicing his instrument, or watching a football band half-time show on TV. The latter asks the student to select the best and the worst moment of some musical event such as a concert or the previous day's rehearsal or music class; what he remembers and how he describes it are clues to his values.

Situations that do not utilize paper and pencil or solicit answers can often yield general information. A check of the *local music stores* and record shops concerning the number of popular and classical records sold to students in a month's time can show something about the relative value each kind of music has for youngsters. A check of the number of students who belong to *church or civic choirs* and instrumental groups can reveal how many value participation enough to pursue it outside the school structure. Purchase of *sheet music* and *recreation instruments* such as ukuleles, *concert attendance,* and viewing of musical *specials* on TV are also indications. *Interviews* with students can offer clues as to their values and attitudes, but one must be systematic and record the events of the interview in the same manner as professional counselors and psychologists gain attitudinal information. *Anecdotal records* of incidents that happened in class or informally and that seem to have significance for the development of values can be written down. As with the psychomotor and cognitive domains, an excellent exercise is to construct sample evaluations for each subdivision of the taxonomy of educational objectives.[25] The taxonomy is presented in Appendix B. Reader identifi-

---

[25] David Krathwohl, ed., *Taxonomy of Educational Objectives: The Classification of Educational Goals, Handbook II: Affective Domain* (New York: David McKay Co., Inc., 1964).

cation and construction of these tools will aid in establishing some acceptable degree of objectivity to this area of music learning. Subjectivity in interpretation is an obstacle in all measurement, but especially in the affective domain. The teacher must be particularly alert to his own biases so that he can try to avoid them and to maintain an objective attitude as he studies the results of evaluative devices. It is tempting to put the right words into the mouths of students, but the safer approach is to look for negative indications and the absence of expected affective learnings, so that more emphasis and better teaching can correct these.

The construction of tools such as those discussed here is a time-consuming activity. Unless they are put together carefully, the information derived from them will be inaccurate and misleading. Criticism and revision are necessary steps in any test construction, and perhaps more important for the affective domain than for skills and knowledge. However, once a satisfactory measure has been constructed it can be used many times for different situations and different students, or even repeated for the same students if comparison is desired. Since attitude tests are not the kind where students may pass on the questions or reveal the answers to others, their usefulness will endure as long as their appropriateness.

QUESTIONS FOR DISCUSSION

1. Discuss the contributions of Kate Gordon Hevner Mueller to evaluation of the affective domain.
2. What effect does the socio-economic background of the students have on teaching and evaluating in the affective domain?
3. Look at some research studies that use a questionnaire and evaluate its adequacy for the stated purposes.
4. Can the schools take credit for teaching anything that cannot be evaluated?
5. Discuss the most important affective objectives for each level of the taxonomy in music education. (See Appendix B.)
6. Identify different methods of evaluation and create sample questions for each level of the taxonomy.

REFERENCES

Anastasi, Anne, *Psychological Testing* (3rd ed.). New York: The Macmillan Company, 1968, Chapter 18.

Berg, Harry, ed., *Evaluation in Social Studies,* Thirty-fifth Yearbook of the National Council for the Social Studies. Washington, D.C.: National Council for the Social Studies, 1965, Chapter 8.

Cronbach, Lee J., *Essentials of Psychological Testing* (3rd ed.). New York: Harper & Row, Publishers, 1970, Part III.

Festinger, Leon, and Daniel Katz, eds., *Research Methods in the Behavioral Sciences.* New York: Holt, Rinehart & Winston, Inc., 1965, Chapter 1.

Gronlund, Norman, *Measurement and Evaluation in Teaching.* New York: The Macmillan Company, 1965, Part IV.

Krathwohl, David, ed., *Taxonomy of Educational Objectives: The Classification of Educational Goals, Handbook II: Affective Domain.* New York: David McKay Co., Inc., 1964.

Oppenheim, A. N., *Questionnaire Design and Attitude Measurement.* New York: Basic Books, Inc., 1966.

Webb, Eugene, et al., *Unobtrusive Measures: Nonreactive Research in the Social Sciences.* Chicago: Rand McNally & Company, 1966, Chapter 8.

CHAPTER EIGHT

published tests

A variety of evaluation tools should be used in any worthy music program. The responsible teacher must be able to select appropriate devices for measuring the results of various experiences in his program. Many important musical behaviors cannot be measured by formal tests, yet published tests should be included as a part of the total program. Published tests tend to be more objective than teacher-constructed devices and are usually more carefully constructed. Standardization implies a body of knowledge and skill that all musically educated children should possess. There are few current worthy tests in music; several have gone out of print recently and few new ones have been added.

This chapter is included to allow the reader: (1) the opportunity to apply what he has learned in other chapters by presenting information from the manuals of tests currently available; (2) the opportunity to judge the purpose, adequacy, and value of each published test in terms of what he has learned about evaluation and to determine what role selected tests might have in a total evaluation program for music. Some of the tests discussed may be judged unworthy of use. In presenting the following list of published tests, the author has attempted to refrain from making value judgments. This is left for a class exercise or for individual evaluation. All information presented has been derived from the test manual or a related publication written by the test author. Purposes are those given by the test author. When items are omitted from the discussion, the test author has either failed to do a thorough job of test construction or has failed to include the information. More information about a test does not imply a better or favored test, only that the information is provided by the test author.

ACHIEVEMENT TESTS
THAT CONTAIN A SOUND RECORDING

Achievement tests are almost nonexistent. The only current tests published by commercial firms are the four *Music Achievement Tests* for elementary, junior and senior high school students, and college elementary education majors and the Aliferis tests for college music majors. Three tests are published by the authors.

Achievement Tests in Music, "Recognition of Rhythm and Melody," William A. Knuth. Creative Arts Research Associates, Monmouth, Oregon. Revised 1967. Divisions I, II, and III, and forms A and B. The student hears a performance of complete musical phrases and is directed to find the error between the notation and the music he has heard. These tests are identical with the original version published in 1936. The 1932 norms are included in the revised edition. A filmstrip is now provided in lieu of the test booklet, and tapes are available, thus eliminating use of the piano.

Validity was established by (1) a detailed textbook analysis of nine well-known public school music series, which identified the various problems of music reading as taught in the public schools; (2) the pooled expert judgment of six music supervisors and college teachers of music education on each of the test items; (3) experimental tryout using 4,208 tests, which secured the percentage of item successes at each consecutive grade level. All schools in the standardization were located in the San Francisco Bay area. Technical data is based on fifty-one students selected at random from each half grade in grades 3 through 8 in each cooperating school. Reliability for division I, grades 3 and 4 is .808; division II, grades 5 and 6, .810; division III, grades 7 and 8, .840. If one gave all three divisions of form A, the reliability is .957. This combined reliability was obtained from scores of students at San Francisco State

College. However, norms are not provided for giving more than one division of the test at a time and are available only for division I at grades 3 and 4, division II for grades 5 and 6, and division III for grades 7 and 8. To obtain percentile scores the user enters the table at the nearest raw score. Only raw scores that correspond to the 10th, 20th, and 30th, etc. percentiles are given. For example, the 50th percentile is equivalent to a score of 12.1 for third-grade students, 13.4 for fifth graders, and 18.7 for seventh graders. Standard deviation is ten to eleven points per test and grade level. Division III provides rough norms for high school students in a cappella choir and glee club, and for brass, woodwind, string, and piano students.

Aliferis Music Achievement Test, James Aliferis. University of Minnesota Press, Minneapolis, Minn., 1954. 28-page manual.

The *Aliferis Music Achievement Test* measures, at the college entrance level (or at the end of high school), the music student's power of auditory-visual discrimination of melodic, harmonic, and rhythmic elements and idioms. The test is given at the piano or on tape and is approximately forty minutes in length. It provides a measure of the student's ability to select from musical notation items he hears played. The author states that this type of experience is commonplace in the everyday world of musical practice and is used in varying degrees by all musicians including composers, performers, conductors, musicologists, and teachers. The original material was gathered from freshman theory and harmony textbooks and by consulting with music instructors. The theory of specifics is applied so that each item of the test might have only one critical problem on which the subject makes a decision.

The element is considered to be the smallest musical unit that could be recognized out of context. The idiom presents each of the elements in a simple context created by grouping two or three elements so as to enlarge the configuration of the one problem contained in the element. The test of melodic elements covers all the intervals from a minor second through the octave. The idioms section presents groups of four tones that incorporate the same intervals. The harmonic elements test covers major and minor chords in all positions of the soprano and bass, and the diminished triad in first inversion. The idioms test presents progressions of three chords including such well-known idioms as II-VI-V-I, the neapolitan cadence, and the deceptive cadence. The rhythmic section contains one-beat rhythmic figures repeated three times in a C-major scale-wise melody. The assumption is that the figure on one beat cannot be recognized when presented singly. Melody is added to avoid the unmusical patterning of rhythms. The piano is used since it is generally accepted by musicians as representative of the complete tonal realm.

The test is designed to be useful for sectioning classes, for comparing individual students, and for analyzing strengths and weaknesses of individual students in melody, harmony, and rhythm. The author believes that a profile using (1) the ear's capacity as shown by the Seashore measures, (2) scores on the Aliferis test, (3) appraisal of the student's performance on his instrument, and (4) appraisal of the student's intellectual capacity would be a reliable profile for determining success as a music student. Criterion-related validity was established by correlating grades of freshman and sophomore students with test scores. The correlation was .61 for 177 freshmen and .53 for 123 sophomores.

Hoyt's method of estimating reliability coefficients was used to obtain a reliability of .88. Subtest reliability was: rhythm .67, harmony .72, and melody .84. Reliability was computed by using 100 test sheets selected at random from 1,768 tests. Item analysis was performed from scores of 100 high and 100 low papers in a random sample from 1,963 answer sheets. The manual contains raw scores, T-scores, and percentile ranks. In the melodic section the mean is about 12.5,[1] with a standard deviation of 6.41. In the harmonic section, the mean is about 7, with a standard deviation of approximately 3.5. The rhythmic section has a mean of about 11, with a standard deviation of 3.5. For the total score, the mean is approximately 31, with the standard deviation approximately 10. Norms are provided by the type of institution, by geographic region, and nationally.

Aliferis-Stecklein Music Achievement Test (College Midpoint Level), James Aliferis and John Stecklein. University of Minnesota Press, Minneapolis, Minn., 1962. 36-page manual.

The test is designed to measure, at the end of the sophomore year, the music student's power of auditory-visual discrimination of melodic intervals, chords, and rhythms. This skill is developed through two classic disciplines, ear training and sight-singing, the importance of which is recognized in that the National Association of Schools of Music (NASM) requires the equivalent of two years of sight-singing and dictation for all

---

[1] Approximations are given since scores are presented by specialized group rather than as one total.

students. For content validity, statements from choral conductors, musicologists, pianists, music educators, composers, and psychologists are quoted. The authors recommend that the test be used to establish school standards, as a basic theory requirement, as objective evaluation over a period of years, for comparison and/or appraisal of a school's achievement with national norms, with like institutions nationally, and with norms for several regions. They also suggest comparable uses for the individual student to examine his own weaknesses and compare his scores with those of others.

Development of the test was similar to that of Aliferis's earlier test. Items were adopted on the basis of item analysis from several trials. The Universities of Minnesota, Michigan, Michigan State, Iowa, Illinois, Ohio State, and Indiana cooperated in the trial editions. Norms are based on scores from 141 member schools of NASM and 2,426 students representing 51 percent of the students completing second-year theory in NASM schools. In the melodic interval section, intervals from the major second through the double octave are included. The student hears a group of four tones. In the test booklet the first three tones are presented and the student selects the fourth tone from four given notes. The chord section contains major and minor, diminished and augmented, augmented sixth, and various types of seventh and ninth chords in all positions of soprano and bass and in closed and open harmony. In taking the test the student looks at a correct chord in the test booklet as he hears a chord, one note of which is wrong. He identifies this error by writing S, A, T, or B for soprano, alto, tenor, or bass. Aliferis contends this testing format is identical with the musician's everyday experience, a continual comparison of the visual and inner ear image of the correct printed page with the mistakes, deviation, and interpretations of the actual sound of music. The rhythm section includes simple and compound meters, rhythmic values as short as thirty-second notes, ties covering two and three beats, ties from whole beats into fractions of the beat, and ties from and into fractional parts of the beat. The student sees the rhythmic group of six beats. He hears the rhythmic group of six beats with one wrong beat, which he identifies. The tempo is established by the use of a tape or, if a tape is unavailable, by the administrator's counting out loud.

Item analyses were made using the test papers of the 500 students with the highest and the 500 students with the lowest total test scores. Aliferis found the discriminative power of the rhythm items low, none exceeding .29, and six with indices between .10 and .19. However, these were considered acceptable in view of the easiness of the items. No single item was marked correctly by more than 79 percent of the students, and at least 40 percent of the group marked all items correctly. Reliability was computed by Kuder-Richardson formula 20 with the 500 high and 500 low papers. Total test reliability is .92, rhythm subtest .69, chord .84, and melody .90. The manual provides part and total intercorrelations. A correlation of .95 between the interval section of the test and the total score of the test is given, indicating one might give only the interval section and obtain a fairly accurate picture of the student's total test score. Criterion-related validity was established by purchasing 400 transcripts of students who had taken the test as sophomores in 1957 and graduated from college by the summer of 1959. Of the 400 transcripts, 226 were usable; that number took all of their work at a single institution. Test scores of applied music majors (N = 56) correlated .51 with grades of all music courses and .51 with grades from all courses at the end of two years. Music education majors' (N = 150) test scores correlated .41 with music courses and .34 with all courses. A similar study was performed using grades for all four years. The author states that correlations of .36 to .40 are an indicator of "predictive" validity. Norms are provided by type of institution, by major instrument, and by geographic region.

Music Achievement Tests, Richard Colwell. Follett Educational Corporation, Chicago, Ill., 1968–70. 36 pages. Administrative and scoring manuals for each of Tests 1–4. A 143-page interpretive manual for tests 1 and 2, 254-page manual for 3 and 4.

These tests consist of four separate tests, each containing three or four subtests of music achievement. They are designed to provide an accurate achievement for some of the most important objectives of the elementary music program. Test 1 covers the area of pitch discrimination, interval discrimination, and meter discrimination. Test 2 includes auditory-visual discrimination, feeling for tonal center, and major-minor mode discrimination. Test 3 consists of tonal memory, melody recognition, pitch recognition, and instrument recognition. Test 4 has subtests on style, texture (monophonic, polyphonic, homophonic), auditory-visual-rhythm, and chord recognition. The author says that the objectives are compatible with any music textbook series, and the test is useful in diagnostic work, program planning, curriculum revision, and evaluation of objectives. Norms are provided for grades 3 through high school.

Purposes are stated as: (1) to determine the extent to which the student has profited from past instruction; (2) to determine the quality of the instruction; and (3) to determine the extent to which students will likely profit from future instruction.

The objectives are: (1) to enable the teacher to determine how well each student has mastered the basic objectives of the school music program; (2) to supply teachers, administrators, parents, and students with information useful in student guidance; (3) to provide teachers and administrators with data for program evaluation and improvement; (4) to provide a teaching device to help the student see clearly some of the objectives of the music program and the nature of his progress with respect to them; (5) to offer information to the instrumental teacher as to those students who might profit from instrumental instruction; and (6) to provide a valid measure for the use of curriculum researchers. Objectives of the various music series are given so that the reader can determine content validity by comparing the objectives of each test with the objectives of the songbooks. Curriculum guides and a conference of elementary music authorities were additional methods used to provide test objectives and content validity. Criterion-related validity was obtained by using teacher ratings of student ability. A correlation of .92 is reported between test scores and ratings based on the top and bottom 20 percent of the class. Predictive validity of MAT has been tentatively established. One study by Edwards gives a correlation of .65 between scores on the test and performance ratings one year later. Correlations between grades given by elementary classroom teachers on song analyses, final grade, class discussions, and test scores were .62, .56, and .64.

Correlations with scores on the *Farnum Music Notation Test* and the Knuth achievement tests in the .5 and .6 range are reported from a small study by Tuley.[2]

Tables of norms include raw score, standard score, and percentile score for each test and subtest by grade level and for combined grades 4, 5, and 6. The composition of the standardization sample, at least 9,000 students for each test is divided by geographical area, type of teacher, size of community, and grade level. Reliability of Test 1 is .94 computed by split-half and .88 computed by KR-21. Standard deviation is 10.41 with a sample size of 7,710. Test 2, with a sample size of 7,894, has a reliability of .942 computed by split-half, .935 by KR-21. The standard deviation is 18.94. Test-retest reliability thirteen days apart was .925, five months apart, .866. KR-14 reliability for Test 3 is .896, Test 4 .898. Reliability estimates computed by KR-21 are given for a sampling of individual rooms and many exceed .90. The mean, standard deviation, reliability, range of scores, standard error of measurement, and median are given by grade level for each test and subtest. Item analysis is provided by grade level; test skewness and kurtosis are given. The mean and standard deviation of each subtest by grade level are given by type of

---

2 Robert Tuley, "A Study of Musical Achievement of Elementary School and Junior High School Pupils at Malcolm Price Laboratory School of the State College of Iowa" (Doctoral dissertation, University of Illinois, 1966).

teacher (music specialist and classroom teacher), sex, geographical area, and size of community.

Musiquiz, William Avar. Period Record Company, Los Angeles, Calif., 1954. 1-page manual.

A record is provided containing selections from twelve overtures. Fourteen possible choices are listed on the answer sheet, and the student matches the title with the selection performed. Included are sections on symphonies, concertos, descriptive pieces, ballet, music of many nations, encores, sounds of the instrument, and miscellaneous. This is the first record of an expected series of ten, which will include 1000 great themes from the famous musical works of all time. The author hopes this will become a national pastime. No norms or other data are provided.

Oberlin Test of Music and Art, no author. Distributed for Oberlin College by the Educational Testing Service, n.d. Contains four forms, A, B, C, D, and a sixteen-page supervisor's manual of instructions. Prepared under a grant from the Ford Foundation and administered at Oberlin about 1960.

The purpose is to determine the effect of college environment on the understanding of art and music. The test requires a tape recorder for music tapes and a slide projector for color slides. There is a short questionnaire about student activities, such as attending concerts and visiting museums. The instructions and the timing are carefully explained in the supervisor's manual. Questions are of the following types: A musical selection is played and several statements are given, e.g., the music was *a Gregorian response, a fifteenth-century motet, a seventeenth-century composition,* or *none of these.* For other questions, the student answers *no statement is false, one statement is false, two, three,* or *four.* Art and architecture questions comprise part of the test. Norms are available from Oberlin College. No technical information is furnished with the test.

Snyder Knuth Music Achievement Test, Alice Snyder Knuth. Cara Publications, Monmouth, Oregon, 1968. Forms A and B. 7-page manual.

This music achievement test is designed to measure an individual's ability to understand musical notation. The test may be used as a placement test at the college and university level to determine the music background of elementary education majors, and it may help determine the need for remedial work prior to elementary music methods. The test may also be useful in measuring the achievement of music majors at both the secondary and college levels. The classroom teacher may also find this test helpful in measuring the musical achievement of girls and boys in the elementary school. Forms A and B are described as equivalent, but no data is provided. Each form is composed of four parts and 136 items: listening and seeing, 53 items; listening, 38 items; musical comprehension, 35 items; and tonal memory, 10 items. The basic elements of music, rhythm, melody, and harmony are not separated but appear as they normally do in music. Folksong material used by children in the public schools is the main source of test item material. The problems are everyday occurrences in the elementary school music program. The author suggests that validity can be checked by looking at courses of study, textbooks, and curriculum guides prepared for teachers in the elementary schools and for teacher-training in colleges. The time for the test is about sixty-five minutes. It is suggested that students scoring less than 80 should probably take a fundamentals course. Reliability of .993 is computed between form A and form B and based on 311 elementary education majors. The correlation between form A and form B for advanced music majors (N = 64) provides a reliability of .998. This extremely high reliability should be carefully checked; reasons can be cited why it might be spuriously high. Additional technical data are available in Mrs. Knuth's dissertation.[3] With 311 elementary education majors, the mean score is 74.65, with a standard deviation of 18.88 for form A; a mean score of 81.46, standard deviation 19.64 is given for form B. For the advanced music major, the mean score of form A is 110.14, standard deviation 12.09; mean of 110.46 and standard deviation 11.17 for form B. Norms are not precisely derived from the scores of the 311 elementary education students, but are based upon the normal probability curve using a mean of 78, standard deviation of 18.00 (an area transformation).

MUSIC ACHIEVEMENT TESTS
REQUIRING A PIANO OR INSTRUMENT

Music Recognition Test, Archie Jones. Carl Fischer, Inc., New York, 1949. 27-page manual consisting of the music. The test has two parts, 80 selections to identify by title in Part I for elementary and junior high

---

[3] Alice Snyder, "The Development, Construction and Standardization of a Test of Music Achievement" (Doctoral dissertation, University of Oregon, 1958).

school, 100 selections to identify in Part II for senior high schools and colleges. A scoring key is provided but no norms or technical data.

The Watkins-Farnum Performance Scale, John Watkins and Stephen Farnum. Hal Leonard Music, Inc., Winona, Minn., 1954 (reprinted 1962). 40-page manual, 33 pages consisting of music for the test.

A standardized achievement test for all band instruments, the scale has as its purpose the measurement of performance and progress on a musical instrument. The authors believe it to be useful in a variety of applications: for testing sight-reading ability, for band tryouts, for seating placement, and for annual or semiannual testing to measure individual improvement. The original cornet scale of Watkins was carefully constructed by analyzing twenty-three widely known methods and obtaining the order in which various music symbols were introduced. Melodies were written to measure sixteen separate levels of achievement. The various symbols of musical notation were introduced according to the order in which they were learned. Criterion-related validity was determined by using rank order correlations. Students were first ranked by their instructors and then by their score on the scale. The correlation between the rankings for clarinet-saxophone was .83, drum .68, cornet .87, flute, oboe, bassoon .86, clarinet and saxophone (group 2) .85, trombone, baritone, tuba .78, trumpet and French horn .77. A standardized method for administering and marking the errors was constructed and the test of seventy-eight exercises was given to 105 cornet students. The difficulty of the exercises was computed and two equivalent forms of fourteen exercises each were made. There is an equal increment of difficulty between each exercise. Forms A and B correlate .982 with each other based on the scores made by the 105 students. Rank order validity coefficients vary from .66 to .91, all except two being above .80. Internal correlations between items and total score range from .44 to .93, over half of these above .80. One hundred fifty-three students took form A (sight-reading), and 71 of these students took form B (practiced performance). Final reliability between the two forms based on students from a wide age span is .953 for sight-reading, .947 for the practiced performance. Farnum obtained a reliability for seventh graders of .87, .94 for tenth- through twelfth- and seventh- through twelfth-grade students. Mean scores range from about 30 for seventh graders to 66 for the high school students, standard deviations range from about 6.3 to 10.4, standard error of measurement from 2.2 to 2.6.

The Farnum String Scale, Stephen Farnum. Hal Leonard Music, Inc., 1969. 28-page manual, 3 pages of which contain instructions and development of the test. Four trial editions were used, each with a few students. A grading chart is furnished based on fourteen of seventeen exercises given to fifty violinists in different sections of the country. No additional data is furnished.

Kwalwasser-Ruch Test of Musical Accomplishment for Grades Four Through Twelve, Jacob Kwalwasser and G. M. Ruch. Bureau of Educational Research and Service, State University of Iowa, Iowa City, Iowa. Revised edition 1927, last reprinted 1952. 8-page manual.

The test is designed to measure the achievement of students in the typical public school music course in elementary and high school. The authors state that every item on the test has been subjected to repeated experimentation and that the items finally included represent materials that public school students reasonably can be expected to master in the course of the first twelve grades of instruction in music. Content validity rests upon the specifications adopted by the *Music Supervisors' National Conference, Bulletin No. 1,* 1921. This bulletin outlined the aims, materials, procedures, and attainments for each of the first eight grades. Validity was further checked against courses of study in Oakland, Pittsburgh, Camden, Evanston, New York, Denver, and others. There are ten subtests: (1) knowledge of musical symbols and terms; (2) recognition of syllable names; (3) detection of pitch errors in a familiar melody; (4) detection of time errors in a familiar melody; (5) recognition of pitch names; (6) knowledge of time signatures; (7) knowledge of key signatures; (8) knowledge of note values; (9) knowledge of rest values; and (10) recognition of familiar melodies from notation. The reliability of the test, .97, is computed by split-half and based on 167 sixth-, eighth-, tenth-, and twelfth-grade students. The standard error of measurement is approximately six score points on either side of the mean. Reliability of the subtests ranges from .70 for knowledge of note values to .97 for knowledge of musical symbols and terms. Percentile scores are based on 5,414 students, grades 4 through 12. They are provided for every 10th percentile, with percentiles for grades 4 through 8. Percentiles for grades 9 through 12 are grouped. The authors defend this by stating that there is little growth in musical accomplishment in these grades.

The Selmer Band Manual Quizzes, Nilo Hovey. H. & A. Selmer Inc., Elkhart, Ind., n.d. 1-page manual.

Seven Selmer band manual quizzes are provided with ten questions on each quiz, five true-false questions, such as "accurate tuning to a single tone is a guarantee that you will play your whole register in tune," four multiple-choice questions, and identification of terms. The quizzes are designed to encourage the student to study this manual objectively and to provide a partial basis for periodic grading of instrumental students. There are no norms or other information.

RESTRICTED TESTS

Three achievement tests are of academic interest only as they are restricted by the publisher and not available for general use. The Committee on Assessing the Progress of Education is preparing the National Assessment of Educational Progress and will have music tests for four age levels, 9, 13, 17, and young adult. The committee represents many of the leaders in evaluation, and one can presume that the tests will be technically well constructed. Hopefully, the music consultants will have provided the guidance to make the questions worthwhile.

The *Graduate Record Examinations* contain *The Advanced Music Test* published by Educational Testing Service, Princeton, N.J. The major content dimensions are grammar of music, theory, instrumentation and orchestration, and history and literature. Two hundred questions comprise this three-hour examination.

The *National Teacher Examinations: Music Education* is another publication of Educational Testing Service. This test contains 125 multiple-choice items and covers all phases of music education: vocal, instrumental, elementary school, and senior high school. Despite the annual revisions of the test, the basic concepts are badly out of date, making the test of little value.

APTITUDE TESTS
THAT CONTAIN A SOUND RECORDING

(Bentley) Measures of Musical Abilities, Arnold Bentley. October House, Inc., New York, 1966. 7-page manual. Research data from his 151-page book.

The battery consists of four tests: pitch discrimination, tonal memory, chord analysis, and rhythmic memory. It is designed for children ages 7–12. The tests purport to measure the kinds of basic judgment that are necessarily involved in music making. The author states that the test may be given to the same children more than once to compensate for minor physical ailments and disturbances. Second testings improve scores about 3 percent, this being attributed to familiarity with the group test situation. The qualification is made in the text that the tests do not measure musical ability in toto because they do not measure intelligence, determination, or industry. The purposes are: (1) a means of assessing a state of readiness for given operations and (2) a general guide in the selection of children for special musical activities requiring more than normal ability. The children who score well on the test are those likely to gain most from more advanced or specialized instruction.

Criterion-related validity was established by comparing test scores with teachers' assessments of the musical capacity of 314 children, rated on a four-point scale. Using the chi-square technique, Bentley established a relationship between the rating and test scores. Scores and ratings of 116 violin students, rated on a four-point progress scale, showed relationship. The tests were administered to musicians, graduates, string teachers, and choral scholars, and they scored well on the battery. A fourth method compared scores with results of an examination used for the selection of boys for choral scholarships in a university college chapel and choir school. The results, based on four groups, confirmed that on all occasions the boys who were quickly eliminated from the competition on the basis of the organist's independent judgment were those who had scored lowest on the test. The correlation with examination scores on sight-reading with 70 boys was .94.

The correlation between I.Q. and subtest scores is in the .20s and .30s. Correlations between interest and test scores are generally in the .30s and .40s. Reliability computed by test-retest over a four-month period with a sample of ninety children is .84. Percentile norms are given in terms of grades comparable to Wing's practice: grade A, the top 10 percent of the students; B, the next 20; grade C, the middle 40; grade D, the next lower 20 percent; and grade E, the lowest 10 percent of the students. The author believes that there are no advantages to providing exact percentiles because this short battery is "no more than a guide, not a revelation of destiny." Percentile grades are provided for ages 7–14. The user is advised to read the book *Musical Ability in Children and Its Measurement* to fully understand the test.

Drake Musical Aptitude Tests, 2nd ed., Raleigh Drake. Science Research Associates, Inc., Chicago, Ill., 1957. 31-page manual.

The tests were designed to provide consistent and valid measures of musical aptitude and to render sound evidence regarding an individual's potential for a successful career in music. The tests can be used with elementary school children, high school youths, college students, and adults. Scores are provided for (1) musical memory and (2) rhythm.

The author believes early discovery of musical aptitude to be more important than early discovery of aptitude in most other fields. He feels that although memory ability can be improved somewhat with training, individual differences are tremendous, as can be verified by any music teacher. Rhythm is included in the test because of the complexity of maintaining accurate rhythm under a number of highly distracting situations. In the rhythm test, a tempo is established and then faded out. The subject continues counting until he is told to stop. He answers by giving the total number of beats that could occur within the time span. "Thus a feeling for rhythm is aroused in the subject and he is allowed to make a musical response to the rhythm." In form B the student must maintain the rhythm in spite of a second distracting tempo; thus, it is more difficult than form A and, Drake believes, usually more valid. The two forms of the rhythm test are not equivalent except in a general way. Forms A and B of the musical memory test are supposedly equivalent. In testing subjects with five or more years musical training, form A of the rhythm tests and either form A or form B of the musical memory test may be omitted. The author believes that if the tests are used as measures of general musical aptitude, they are highly valid in terms of predicting success in music training. A person's interest in music or a highly specific aptitude for particular kinds of performance is not measured.

The musical memory test consists of two-bar melodies, which are to be remembered and compared with a series of two-bar melodies for possible changes in time, key, or note. 5,894 cases were used for the musical memory norms, 2,830 for the rhythm norms. Since the testing was done in England, Belgium, India, and the United States, it is claimed that the test is culture free. Music teacher ratings of individual students was the method of obtaining criterion-related validity on the test. On a seven-point rating scale, correlation coefficients were obtained ranging from .31 to .91, with a majority greater than .58. The author states that these compare favorably with those of many individually administered intelligence tests, using similar methods for establishing criterion-related validity. With two groups, he was able to obtain a second rating to measure the reliability of the raters. With one group of thirteen and another of thirty-eight, the correlation between ratings was .68. Uniquely, he obtained a higher reliability for homogeneous groups than for those with wide heterogeneity. Reliability coefficients based on scores of persons with musical training are in the .90s, those with untrained personnel are lower, mostly in the .70s and .80s. Split-half reliability by groups computed using both forms of the musical memory test is .91, .85, and .93. The reliability of the rhythm test is reported based on ten groups and ranges from .56 to .96, with the average in the .80s.

Correlations between the two tests are low, and correlations between the test score and age are also low. In the musical memory test, there are generally about 1.8 fewer mistakes with each increasing year of age. Using four groups of musical and nonmusical students, the correlation with the amount of musical training was low, ranging from about .32 to .43. Drake says this indicates "pure" aptitude and not achievement. There is a slight superiority for girls in music memory (1½ points per test), but this is not reflected in the norms. Scores are not related to college grades; in other words, Drake states that the ordinary factor of motivation and learning ability is not making the difference in scores. Scores are not related to intelligence.

Norms for the rhythm test are the same for all ages, but differ for music and nonmusic students. Music memory norms are given separately for form A, form B, and forms A and B for music and nonmusic students. One can miss many questions and score acceptably. For example, a fourth-grade student can miss 74 of 106 questions and be at 50th percent level; 20-year-olds can miss 46 and score at the 50th percentile. The chance factor is a major one.

Farnum Music Test, Stephen E. Farnum. Bond Publishing Company, Riverside, R.I., 1969. 15-page manual.

The purpose of the test is to select beginners for all musical instruments, and Farnum considers the test a predictive measure. A recording is provided. Complete testing time recommended is between forty and fifty minutes. Farnum identified four important factors from a pilot study with 170 high school music students: (1) eye and hand coordination (symbol digit test); (2) recognition of music notation (the former *Farnum Music Notation Test*); (3) tests of musical memory (tonal patterns); and (4) tonal movement (cadence). The musical memory test is based on the Seashore "Tonal Patterns Test," and the tonal movement section is based upon the Kwalwasser-Dykema "Tonal Movement Test." Validity was established by comparing the test scores of 152 children, with scores on the *Watkins-Farnum Performance Scale*. Correlation coefficient was .63. In computing this, the last two tests (musical memory and tonal movement) are given only half weight. Reliability is provided for the symbol test only; test-retest, $N = 70$, .87 and $N = 77$, .91. No norms or other technical data are provided.

Kwalwasser Music Talent Test, Jacob Kwalwasser. Mills Music, Inc., New York, 1953. 4-page manual.

The author states that where great differences in scores are found between individuals, the difference is due to superior equipment on the part of the superior individual and is unlikely to be linked with training, intelligence, sex, or nationality.[4] He does not believe teachers can increase a child's potential "one iota." All the teacher can do is use the native capacity possessed by the child. He believes this to be the major reason for music talent testing. The test takes ten minutes to administer. Form B is not as difficult as form A and is not a comparable form. Form A consists of fifty three-tone patterns, which are repeated with possible variation in either pitch, time, rhythm, or loudness. The student decides whether the repeated pattern is the same or different. Percentile scores for form B are presented for grades 4, 5, and 6 (grouped) including a 100 percentile for scores of 35 and above and a 0 percent for 13 and below; the 100 and 0 percentiles are impossible. Form A provides one set of percentile scores for grades 7–9 (grouped) and one for senior high school and college (grouped).

K-D Music Tests, Jacob Kwalwasser and Peter W. Dykema. Carl Fisher, Inc., New York, 1930; copyright renewed. 34-page manual.

The purposes of the test are not given. A ranking is provided that is presumably a percentile based on the number of right answers in each part of the test. The ten subtests are tonal memory, quality, intensity, tonal movement, time, rhythm, pitch, taste, pitch imagery, and rhythm imagery. Ranks are provided from 0 to 100, the 0 and the 100 are impossible. Ranks for each of ten tests, and for the total test, are provided for combined grades 4, 5, and 6; 7, 8, and 9; and 10, 11, and 12. No technical information is furnished.

Musical Aptitude Profile, Edwin Gordon. Houghton Mifflin Company, Boston, 1965. 113-page manual.

The basic factors of musical aptitude are considered by Gordon to be musical expression, aural perception, and kinesthetic musical feeling. The stated major purpose of the profile is "to act as an objective aid in the evaluation of students' basic musical aptitude so that the teacher can better provide for individual needs and ability."[5] Other purposes are: (1) to encourage musically talented students to participate in music performance organizations; (2) to adapt music instruction to meet the individual needs and ability of students; (3) to formulate educational plans

---

[4] Jacob Kwalwasser, *Kwalwasser Music Talent Test,* "Instruction Manual" (New York: Mills Music, Inc., 1953), p. 3.

[5] Edwin Gordon, *Musical Aptitude Profile,* "Manual" (Boston: Houghton Mifflin Company, 1965), p. 2.

in music; (4) to evaluate the music aptitude of groups of students; and (5) to provide parents with objective information. The test is divided into three main divisions: tonal imagery, rhythm imagery, and musical sensitivity. Tonal imagery has two parts, memory and harmony. Rhythm imagery is divided into tempo and meter. Musical sensitivity consists of three preference subtests, phrasing, balance, and style. The author states the seven areas probably do not represent all areas of musical aptitude, but the test user must have confidence that these areas are capable of reflecting musical aptitude. He suggests that the test user depend heavily upon subjective judgments of the rationale for the test and the evidence concerning test content and methodology. A correlation study with teachers' rating was performed. Teachers in two schools rated students in five categories: highest 10 percent; above average, next 15 percent; average, 50 percent; below average, 15 percent; and the lowest 10 percent. This is presented by groups such as high school band, high school choir, junior high school band, etc. With total score, the correlations range from .64 to .97 (the highest was eighteen members of a junior high boys glee club). Correlations are generally in the high 70s and low 80s. With one teacher who Gordon felt knew the students quite well, the correlations ranged from .53 to .72. Other studies are reported with correlations between music performance scores (obtained from the ratings of three judges) and test scores ranging from .12 to .43.

The complete test is 115 minutes in length, with the recommendation for administration in three 50-minute periods. Four revisions are reported with one complete school system providing data for each revision. Schools participating in the norming were selected by the method employed in Project Talent. Elementary and junior high schools that were feeder schools for the senior high school, with approximately the same number of students in each of grades 4 through 12, were used. 12,809 students from twenty school systems in eighteen states comprised the standardization sample. The schools represent one large city, one suburb, and eighteen small towns. Research has been conducted using the test with both younger and older students.

Reliability coefficients were computed by the split-half method and range on total tests from .90 to .96 for the different grade levels. Reliabilities are in the .60s and .70s for the subtest and generally in the .80s for the major divisions. Test-retest reliability (one year apart) is .80, with subtests in the 50s. Mean, standard deviation, and standard error of measurement are given for each subtest by grade level and for combined grades (combined by elementary school, junior, and senior high school). Intercorrelations among subtests are generally in the .70s and .80s. These intercorrelations are given for grades 5, 8, and 11. Mean item analysis is furnished by grouped grades, elementary, and junior and senior high school.

The effect of one semester of musical training on test scores was negligible on each year of a three-year study; the improvement of scores was between 3 and 4 percent. Correlation of scores with intelligence is positive and moderately high; for fourth- through sixth-grade students, .58; for seventh- and eighth-grade students, .48, a composite of .56. Correlation with the *Iowa Tests of Educational Development* was .43.

Predictive validity was established by an unusual experiment, in which all students in selected schools studied instrumental music for three years. Correlations between teacher ratings and expert ratings on performance with test scores are given in "A Three Year Study of the Musical Aptitude Profile."[6] These correlations encompass a wide range. When using the manual, standard scores must be used in order to determine percentile scores. A characteristic of the Gordon test is the apparent ease of obtaining a respectable score, since the middle norms of fourth-grade students are very close to chance. A difference of two or three raw score points above chance in the tonal imagery and rhythmic imagery sections places the student at the 50th percentile; with the three preference tests, five points above chance can place a student at the 60th percentile of the national norms. For this reason care must be taken when using the test in following directions exactly and in interpreting the results. A "good" day or a "bad" day could have a marked effect upon test scores. This situation is often necessary with a test designed for all students and a wide age range.

Musical Talent Test, no author. F. E. Olds and Sons, Fullerton, Calif., n.d. No manual.

The test contains five sections of five questions each: pitch (same or different), time (which is faster), harmony (which sounds best), intensity (which tone is louder), and rhythm (same or different). A second portion contains a short section that allows the teacher to rate teeth, mouth, lips, fingers, and to make a general recommendation. An arbitrary score of 68 or above for nine- to twelve-year-old students has been established as being excellent; for thirteen- to sixteen-year-olds, 80 or above is excellent; and for seventeen- to twenty-year-olds, 92 or above is excellent. A fair score for nine- to twelve-year-olds is 44–52. A score of 48 is possible by chance.

---

[6] Edwin Gordon, "A Three Year Study of the Musical Aptitude Profile," *Studies in the Psychology of Music,* Vol. V (Iowa City: University of Iowa Press, 1967).

The Seashore Measures of Musical Talent, Carl Seashore, Don Lewis, Joseph Saetveit. The Psychological Corporation, New York, 1960 revision. 11-page manual.

Seashore states that "one important area of ability not tapped by typical scholastic or general aptitude tests is that of musical ability."[7] The uses for the test are given as educational and vocational counseling, admission to musical instruction in schools, and selection for membership in bands and other musical organizations. The authors state that not all the facets of musical aptitude are known but there are several fundamental capacities that can be assessed. The six Seashore capacities are pitch, loudness, rhythm, time, timbre, and tonal memory. The original tests, published in 1919, were unchanged for twenty years. The 1939 revisions improved the precision of the stimuli, and the timbre test replaced the consonance test. The 1960 revision did not alter the test content but made it available on LP records.

In the pitch test, fifty pairs of tones are presented; the student determines whether the second tone is higher or lower than the first. The same number and type of task are required on the loudness, rhythm, and timbre tests. In the rhythm and tonal sequence tests there are thirty pairs of patterns. In the tonal sequence test the student determines which note is changed.

Norms are presented for three levels. Levels were chosen rather than single grades because differences among the adjacent grades were generally too small to warrant norms for each grade. The levels are grades 4 and 5, grades 6 through 8, and grades 9 through 16. Sex differences were too small and inconsistent from one level to another to report. Norms are not given for the total test; each section is evaluated separately.

Seashore always steadfastly maintained that the tests' internal validity was well established and that attempts to validate them against fallible external criterion measures such as judgments of omnibus musical behavior were inappropriate. He held that he had isolated pitch among all other factors, and no scientist would question the fact that he has measured pitch discrimination. A detailed account of the content, construction, and analysis of the test is found in a report by Saetveit, Lewis, and Seashore entitled "Revision of the Seashore Measures of Musical Talent."[8]

---

7 Carl Seashore, Don Lewis, and Joseph Saetveit, *The Seashore Measures of Musical Talents,* Manual (New York: The Psychological Corporation, 1960), p. 3.

8 Saetveit, Lewis, and Seashore, "Revision of the Seashore Measures of Musical Talent," *University Iowa Studies, Aims, Prognosis,* Research Number 65 (Iowa City: University of Iowa Press, 1940).

The Stanton studies, covering a ten-year period at the Eastman School of Music, appeared to confirm the validity of the Seashore measures, but the scores were coupled with intelligence test scores and tonal imagery test scores for prediction purposes. Stanton stated that the fact that Eastman graduates did not improve their Seashore scores over a four-year period was proof that the test measured aptitude. Possibly, their entering scores were so near the top that no practical room for improvement remained.

The reliability of the Seashore measures was estimated by using KR-21. The coefficients of reliability for grades 4 and 5 were: pitch .82, loudness .85, rhythm .87, time .72, timbre .55, tonal memory .81. For grades 6 through 8 the coefficients were .84, .82, .69, .63, .63, .64 respectively, and for grades 9 through 16, .84, .74, .64, .71, .68, .83 for the six subtests. The user is cautioned that when the coefficients are low, one should interpret in broad categories or the student should be retested. Norms give only raw and percentile scores. The size of sample (N), the mean, and the standard deviation are given for each section and for each grade level. Twelve public schools were used for the standardization, providing data on from less than 400 students for some subtests and levels to more than 4000 for the oldest level.

The Selmer Music Guidance Survey.

This is entitled a survey rather than an examination, test, or quiz because students might have an unpleasant connection with tests. The rationale is that perhaps the most important attribute in learning to play a musical instrument is desire on the part of the student. Any action that might lessen this desire at the outset would certainly be unwise. Students are informed that the survey is to guide the instrumental teacher in selecting the right instrument and that the results in no way affect his scholastic records or his possibilities in instrumental music. The test contains sixteen items on pitch recognition (higher, same or lower), sixteen items on chordal memory (same or different), twelve items on melody memory (same or different), and sixteen items on rhythm memory (same or different). A scoring key is provided but no norms or other information for the teacher.

The Standardised Tests of Musical Intelligence, Herbert Wing. National Foundation for Educational Research (England and Wales), The Mere, Upton Park, Slough, Buckinghamshire, England. Most technical information contained in *Tests of Musical Ability and Appreciation,* 2nd ed.,

Cambridge University Press, Cambridge, England, 1968. In this text the test is also entitled *Wing Musical Aptitude Test.*

Wing hopes to satisfy both the musician and the psychologist in providing a means for assessing the musical capacity of individual subjects, especially those of school age. He investigated a mode of selecting children who would be suitable for training on a musical instrument as well as providing vocational guidance for those who might like to follow music as a profession. He believes musical appreciation is the power to recognize or evaluate artistic merit in music and that it involves deliberate aesthetic judgment of music; this differs from musical ability although they may be connected in some manner. Wing tried several tests but limited the final form to 160 items in seven categories. They are (1) chord analysis, detecting the number of notes played in a single chord; (2) pitch change, detecting the alteration of a single note in a repeated chord; (3) memory, detecting the alteration of a note in a short melody; (4) rhythmic action, choosing the better rhythmic accent of two performances; (5) harmony, judging the more appropriate of two harmonizations; (6) intensity, judging the more appropriate mode of varying loudness (crescendo-decrescendo) in two performances of the same melody; and (7) phrasing, judging the more appropriate phrasing. The test takes fifty minutes. Wing's research sample was evenly distributed with respect to training and home background. Wing finds improvement to be not more than 4 percent on a second administration of the test. The correlation with general intelligence is .3. Dropouts were computed on 333 boys, ages 14 through 16. Of the eighty-four children in the A-B category only 2 percent dropped out of music, but of those in the D and E category (N = 100) 40 percent dropped. He feels that it would be better to discourage those of low musical capacity from commencing the study of an instrument. The test-retest reliability of thirteen tests was .95 using seventy-one boys (aged 15), and with the present seven tests it was .91 based on a group of forty-one boys and a group of sixty-five boys. Reliability coefficient of test-retest over four years is .77. The reliability of the first three tests is .89 and the four preference tests .84, with a sample of forty-one students. The author says that this reliability is as high as can be expected of a test concerned with the aesthetics of music. By totaling the scores of each test a musical quotient can be obtained by use of a graph or simple formula. To obtain criterion-related validity, Wing correlated scores with rankings of three teachers. These correlations were .64, .78, and .82.

Percentile scores are based mainly on schools in various districts of London, but in comparisons of these with other schools in England little difference was found. The standardization sample was 3,373 using as few as 67 nine-year-olds but ranging up to 561 thirteen-year-olds. Wing has data on about 8000 students, but it is not at all clear from the manual whether the additional data are used in any of the technical considerations. He states, "The norms for the first three tests are not changed to any marked extent," while norms for the total test have reduced totals. He suggests that grades be computed on the basis of the top 10 percent, A; next 20 percent, B; the next 40 percent, C; next 20 percent, D; and the bottom 10 percent, E. Score evaluation by these letter grades are the norms and are provided for combined tests 1, 2, and 3 and for total test. He feels a more exact delineation by percentiles will give a false idea of accuracy. Sex was an insignificant factor in scores on this test. The correlation between interest and ability is about .30. Item analysis is not given but was used to shorten the test in the revised edition.

A Test of Musicality, E. Thayer Gaston, 4th ed. Revised manual. Odell's Instrumental Service, Lawrence, Kan., 1957. 20-page manual.

The test has been devised to secure information regarding the musical personality of the child or student tested. The purpose is to ascertain both directly and indirectly the drawing power or valence of music for the individual and to show his awareness of tonal-rhythmic configurations and his response thereto. Test parts include attitude, pitch identification, tonal imagery, tonal completion, and tonal memory. Gaston believes that the musicality of the average child is not directly dependent upon separate sensory abilities, but is dependent upon his interaction with items of musical influence in his environment. There are probably certain unique hereditary factors, but they are of no greater importance than environmental factors may be. It is the child's perceptual rather than his sensory ability that is essential, and the chief factor in musicality is an awareness of relatedness among tones. Consequently, since melody is the primary musical phenomenon, melodic apprehension and response may be considered to have high diagnostic significance. Information provided by the music teacher is important in making a valid judgment on the musical personality of the students. The test is based upon Gaston's twenty years of teaching experience and his six years of experimentation and measurement of attitudes, potentialities, and performance of school children in their musical activities. He says he studied the qualifications and characteristics of 15,000 students, third grade through the senior university year. The test was first given to 1200 fifth- to twelfth-grade students in four different school systems. Several minor revisions were made, and it was then administered to 4,840 students from twenty-six schools in seven different states for his norming sample. Criterion-related validity of the test was established by teacher rating, using five categories: poor, below average, average, good, and excellent. The sample is 653 students in grades 4 through 6 and 153 students in grades 10, 11, 12. The results show a correlation between scores and ratings. Split-half reliability for 653 fourth- through sixth-grade students and 166 seventh- through ninth-grade students is .88; it is .90 for 153 students in grades 10, 11, and 12. The inventory for liking of music is scored as part of the test. Percentile scores are provided for grades 5 through 8 grouped. Boys in grade 4 score higher than boys in grades 5 through 8 at the 10th through the 70th percentiles; only at the 80th and 90th percentiles do older boys excel. Sex norms are provided by grouping boys grades 4 through 8 and 9 through 12. The same procedure is followed for the girls. Sex norms are also provided for boys and girls separately for grades 4 through 6, 7 and 8, 9 and 10, and 11 and 12. Another table of norms is given for boys and girls separated for ages 9 through 11, 12 and 13, 14 and 15, 16 through 18. The norming sample has as few as fifty-one boys age 9 and 64 girls of that age.

Tilson-Gretsch Musical Aptitude Tests, Lowell M. Tilson. The Fred Gretsch Mfg. Co., 1941. The manual is a reprint from the *Teachers College Journal,* May 1941, entitled "A Study of the Prognostic Value of the Tilson-Gretsch Musical Aptitude Tests." 3-page manual.

These musical aptitude tests were constructed for the purpose of furnishing a battery of tests for a quick and accurate survey of the musical possibilities in elementary and secondary school children. It was not the intention of the author to produce a battery of tests that would be sensitive enough to select special music students for music education curriculum in colleges and universities. The test has four sections, pitch, intensity, time, and tonal memory, each similar to the Seashore tests.

Validity is based on grouping of students into four talent categories by teachers. Ninety-two percent of students in the lowest talent group made grades below the median; 55 percent were below the first quartile and only 5 percent above the third quartile. Of students in the highest quarter of talent, 35 percent scored below the median, 8 percent below the first quartile, and 56 percent above the third quartile.

APTITUDE TESTS
REQUIRING A PIANO OR MUSICAL INSTRUMENT

The Biondo Music Aptitude Test, "A Musical Quiz," C. A. Biondo. (A recruiting aid for orchestras and bands.) Scherl and Roth, Inc., Cleveland, Ohio. Reprinted from C. A. Biondo, *Starting the Instrumental Program* (Gregorian Institute of America, Toledo, Ohio), 1957. 3-page manual.

The author states that the battery was devised for use by string and band teachers as a recruiting aid for the instrumental program. The test is standardized with 1000 third-, fourth-, and fifth-grade children in South Bend, Indiana. The string recruiter should administer the test on the violin, and the band recruiter may use the clarinet. The teacher should have at least two trial runs so the subjects know how to listen and how to mark the test blanks. The test is comprised of two subtests, thirty-two pitch items (higher and lower), and twenty-four items in a rhythm memory test (same or different).

Raw scores and percentile scores for third-, fourth-, and fifth-grade are given. Scores on the two tests are not combined.

The Leblanc Music Talent Quiz, ed. E. C. Moore. G. Leblanc Company, Kenosha, Wis., 1954. 4-page manual.

In the manual it is stated that in giving the Leblanc quiz the instructor should be careful to avoid the appearance of giving a test or an examination. Rather, he would do best, perhaps, to open with an informal talk on the instruments of the band and orchestra. The director is advised to make it a "good time session with emphasis on the fun in music, yet maintaining the proper control." It is further recommended that one may find it good psychology to offer some little prize or prizes for the highest scores. The test contains six sections with fifty pairs of notes or groups of notes in (A) rhythm patterns, (B) melody retention, (C) interval recognition, (D) chord retention, (E) pitch recognition, and (F) chord recognition. Answers are *same or different* or *higher or lower.* No means, percentiles, or other information are available. The talent quiz is based on experience Mr. Moore has gained during thirty-five years of teaching at all four levels. The rationale is that the talent test should never be used to discourage children from trying to play an instrument. The tests "are best used to give encouragement to the child and to show parents that every girl or boy can learn to play an instrument and should be given every opportunity to enjoy a musical education."

Music Aptitude Test, no author. Pan American Band Instruments, a division of the C. G. Conn Company, Elkhart, Ind., 1951. 25-page manual.

The rationale is that the gift for music is largely an interest in music. The test has sections on rhythm (*same or different*), tempo (*same or different*), pitch (*same or different*), and pitch (*up or down*), each of five items. In the first melody test (five items), the student determines *same or different;* in a second, the determination is *correct or incorrect.* A *same-different* and an *up or down* chord test completes this section. A vision test is provided in which the examiner uses a baton and conducts patterns twice, and the student must tell whether the patterns are the same or different. Last is a mathematics test in which a number of fingers are held up on one hand and on the other, and the student must add them together. No technical information is available, although it is suggested that 2 on a test is poor, 4 good, and 5 perfect. Part of the manual describes letters and other promotion items that can be sent home to encourage students to join the band.

APTITUDE TESTS, PAPER AND PENCIL

Music Listening Evaluation Form, F. Anthony Viggiano. Wm. C. Brown Company, Publishers, Dubuque, Iowa, 1956, 1958.

This is a listening check sheet on which the student is able to record what he hears, his general impression, prominent solo passages, instruments used, and his reaction; he can make a selection from three adjectives that describe the music.

QUESTIONS FOR DISCUSSION

1. Evaluate each test as to its:
   (a) adequacy of construction: reliability, validity, usefulness, usability, research, and necessary technical data
   (b) norming procedures
   (c) grade level appropriateness
2. Plan the use of standardized tests in a six-year music program. Specify frequency, time of administration, and purpose of the test.

REFERENCES

Buros, Oscar K., *Mental Measurements Yearbooks*. Highland Park, N.J.: The Gryphon Press, 1965. Issued at five-year intervals.

————, *Tests in Print: A Comprehensive Bibliography of Tests for Use in Education, Psychology, and Industry.* Highland Park, N.J.: The Gryphon Press, 1961.

Lehman, Paul, *Tests and Measurements in Music.* Englewood Cliffs, N.J.: Prentice-Hall, Inc., 1968.

Wheeler, Pat, ed., Bimonthly newsletter of new tests received. Princeton, N.J.: Carl Campbell Brigham Library of Educational Testing Service.

APPENDIX
A

application of the taxonomy of psychomotor objectives

Professor Simpson's basic category in the psychomotor domain is perception (1.0), with subdivisions of sensory stimulation (1.1), cue selection (1.2), and translation (1.3). There is some question as to whether 1.2 and 1.3 should not be at a higher level, perhaps between 3.0, guided response, and 4.0, mechanism. Secondly, auditory-perceptual skill, a major part of the musical act, fits only in the perceptual category of the taxonomy and yet seems to encompass a wide range of difficulty. For example, cue selection may include acts as simple as mentally hearing and then reproducing a single tone and acts as highly complex as recognizing registration in organ music or sensing the proper articulation and phrasing from auditory cues. A good case can be made for the need to develop a separate taxonomy in the perceptual domain.

Because of this ambiguity in the present taxonomy examples are given only for categories 2.0 on.

Set (2.0) is readily recognizable as the preparatory adjustment or readiness for a particular act or experience. Set may be mental (2.1), physical (2.2), or emotional (2.3). Mental set implies having the relevant knowledge for the task. Before the student can execute a certain musical act, whether playing an instrument, following the oboe melody in a symphonic movement, or analyzing a piece of music for its form, he has to have the requisite mental equipment—the knowledge of how to finger and blow the instrument, the knowledge of how the oboe timbre sounds, or the knowledge of music reading and formal structure. For playing the instrument he would also have to have a physical set involving proper posture, instrument position, embouchure formation, and the intake of air by use of the diaphragm. Following the oboe melody would perhaps not entail any physical set, although attentive listening is promoted by a posture that is not too relaxed. Emotional set is also familiar to the teacher; it appears to have two facets. One kind of emotional set is a willingness or readiness for the task, an affirmative response to the idea of the task. The second kind of emotional set so common to music is the "feeling" one has for a march, for a waltz, for the sound of the violin or a trumpet. In thinking about these musical specifics, we can observe that we have a different emotional response to each that is partly a kinesthetic quality but also imaginative and emotional. Interestingly, the set of hearing a pitch before producing it seems to include all three categories of set: it is primarily a mental act, but includes an element of physical set and also a certain emotional quality that varies from pitch to pitch.

Evaluation of physical set is important in music and relatively simple. The teacher can see whether the conducting student is physically ready to begin the upbeat or preparatory beat, or whether the singer is physically prepared to begin the opening phrase of the song. This evaluation is especially useful in beginning string instruction, where the player must be both alert and relaxed, his fingers in position to produce not only the correct pitch but the correct quality of tone, with the bow arm's position equally important. In string playing, physical set may be one of the most vital areas for evaluation; the teacher's emphasis upon tension, relaxation, and free movement is basically an effort to produce a continuous proper physical set because this is essential to good playing. Pianists are also concerned with physical set, though to a lesser extent than string players. The position of the hand over the keys and the positions of the arms, elbows, shoulders, and back all contribute to the pianist's control. A careful look at the performer can help an experienced teacher evaluate many elements of physical set. However, use of photographs or video tapes can illustrate to the player where his errors are and what should be done to correct them in the interest of better performance.

Guided response (3.0) as an objective in the psychomotor domain means that this is one stage of learning that the student should attain. The learner advances by the methods of imitation (3.1) or trial and error (3.2.) Imitation is used in music at every level, from the kindergarten teacher introducing a new four-measure song to the distinguished conductor coaxing an interpretation of a symphonic passage from his orchestra. Imitation is perhaps the most effective form of teaching and learning in musical performance. The bassoon teacher says, "Now listen to how this passage sounds when I play it," and the student understands more vividly than if the teacher explained for the entire lesson. This approach is used continually and with success.

Trial and error as a form of learning or as an objective is most frequently found in musical composition or other creative activities such as conducting, moving to music, orchestration, or playing by ear. Learning to produce a good tone can also be accomplished by trial and error if the player or singer knows how to listen carefully to himself. He may not have a teacher who can demonstrate good tone, and he may not have access to recordings that illustrate desirable quality for him, but through the process of trial and error plus careful listening he can arrive at acceptable or even outstanding tone quality.

The effects of trial and error or imitation can be judged by using a tape recorder. The effects of guided response as a teaching-learning process can only be determined with reference to the curriculum objectives—whether this approach is appropriate to reach some of the stated objectives. Trial and error can be very wasteful of time and energy as well as discouraging, and imitation can lead to dependence and weakness, as for example the skillful organist who says, "I always take lessons when I want to learn new music; it's so much easier to let the teacher tell you how to do it than to figure it out for yourself." Where the objectives warrant guided response and the teacher is experienced in using it to good advantage, then its use is appropriate.

Mechanism (4.0) is the level of psychomotor skills at which the learned response has become habitual and can be performed with a minimum of thought for the skill process itself. In music, mechanism means that the performer has a repertoire of skills that he can use in response to the demands of any situation. Such items as scales and chords, different types of embouchure, different kinds of touch for the pianist and bowing for the string player, and different vocal sounds for the singer are part of the repertoire the performer uses. If perfect pitch can be learned or relative pitch improved, acuteness of discrimination in ear training is also a mechanism. These are acquired through drill and practice. Exercises, warm-ups, vocalises, lip slurs, and similar items are designed to accomplish the objective of mechanism. Evaluation is pertinent to these techniques and others: how to breathe correctly, how to double tongue, which fingers should be used, where to facilitate intonation or flexibility, how to change registers. Because evaluation is limited to observation, a variety of approaches to observing and recording the students' skills is valuable. Each skill should be listed and students should be evaluated periodically on each. The idea cannot be supported that in the course of a year the alert teacher will somehow naturally make systematic observations on each aspect of each student's development. On any one instrument or voice, the skill aspects are too numerous to remember for each student without written record. The teacher may recognize some weaknesses and gaps but fail to help the student correct them when there is no systematic evaluation, and other weaknesses may go completely unnoticed. Inhaling, exhaling, tone, attacks, range, quality, releases, flexibility, tension, embouchure, fingering patterns, aural perception, etc. are each important. Systematic evaluation will not only aid in focusing the learner's practice but will become a determining factor in the selection of materials and exercises for each individual. All learning is individual but skill learning may be even more influenced by individual differences than the acquisition of cognitive learning. For this reason the teacher needs to know how each student is progressing and make individual assignments accordingly.

Complex overt response (5.0) is the final level of psychomotor objectives with which the teacher need be concerned. Here the student can perform with a high degree of skill a task involving a variety of motor acts. The individual proceeds with confidence having arrived at the resolution of uncertainty (5.1). He can, for example, accurately read at sight a piece of music that demands response to meter symbol, key signature, pitch and rhythm symbols, expression marks, tempo marks, and phrasing, commanding the motor skills required by each. In listening he can identify major melodies and motifs, supporting or subsidiary melodies, instruments in combination or alone, various kinds of cadence, key relationships, repetition, imitation, variation, and contrast, using these to help in following and understanding the music. Simpson labels this automatic performance (5.2), for most of the skills come upon command, without hesitation or special effort.

The two levels of adaptation and origination (6.0) and (7.0) are seen as tentative by Simpson. They seem to be valid levels for the development of musical skills, but depend upon the creative insight of the performer himself, rather than upon the guidance of a teacher. Simpson suggests that adapting and originating may be possible at all levels, even the simplest; if this is true, it is also true by definition that these acts come from within the individual rather than from the outside. If imposed, it is the teacher rather than the learner who is doing the adapting and creating; therefore, these cannot be planned for as levels of development but merely guided and fostered when they occur.

Each area discussed above in the taxonomy of musical skills includes acts ranging from simple to complex. There is a hierarchy of difficulty within each level as well as between levels. Teachers need to be aware of this in setting up objectives and planning techniques of evaluation. If students must be free to develop in whichever manner chance happens to dictate, the teacher's role is little more than that of a monitor or a resource person. However, individual development can be tolerated and even planned for if a systematic program is available for recording individual achievement so that growth can be well rounded and focused, materials and learning experiences controlled, each student recognized and considered.

APPENDIX
B

a taxonomy
of objectives
for the affective domain

1.0 Receiving. Receiving is obviously the prerequisite for any kind of positive response, since no impression can be made upon the student who is not receptive. Since one of the unique characteristics of the affective domain is that conformity cannot be imposed or forced, a receptive posture must be elicited from the student before any progress can begin.

1.1 Awareness. Awareness is very close to cognition; it is more mental than emotional. It is not based upon recall as a cognitive act would be, but is a state of being conscious to outside forces. More diffuse than attention, awareness may not contain recognition of specifics but does take into account the situation or phenomenon. Questions in music directed toward awareness might ask the student to raise his hand when there was a definite change in the music being played on a record—different instruments, different section, different meter, etc. Mood questions might also be appropriate for this level: Does the piece sound happy or sad? stately or playful? Mood is a sufficiently obvious quality that controlled attention is usually not necessary for recognition.

1.2 Willingness to receive. This level differs from the previous one in that the passivity has opened up to show some consent. The student is still neutral but can be given ideas, direction, explanation, or emotional tones without showing rejection or negative response. Information about the various kinds of music can be tested for as a clue to development of this level. If the student has retained some concepts of what makes classical music treasured and how it differs from commercial or folk or current pop music, he shows a willingness to receive. Attitude questions might be asked with some success, such as "Would you go to a cello concert if you had never been to one before?" or "Which of the following is the (a) most attractive to you? (b) least attractive to you? (c) most familiar? (d) least known?: Beethoven's Fifth Symphony, 'I Get By With a Little Help From My Friends,' 'Dixie,' 'St. Louis Blues,' 'Waltz of the Flowers' . . ." "Would you be interested in: learning to play the piano? singing in a school choir? learning to play in a band? playing the guitar?" Willingness to receive can also be explored at the adult level for the introduction of new ideas about music and music teaching. Attitude questions for teachers might include: "Are you willing to consider changing the instrumental music curriculum? Will you attend a one-hour weekly committee meeting for this purpose? Will you read one book or pamphlet a week on the subject?"

1.3 Controlled or selected attention. A step above willingness to receive is selected attention; here the student is sufficiently active to focus upon certain aspects of his own choosing rather than depending solely upon the teacher's suggestions. This level may thus be seen as the first step in an active relationship with music, although the action is no more than directing the attention to more favored stimuli. Questions can now take the form of specifying the instruments heard or telling why one part of the music sounds different from a previous part or determining whether the meter moves in duple or triple. Such questions have a large proportion of cognition, but their main purpose is response to the music. Attitude or preference questions could ask the student to choose which of several compositions he likes the best or which version of a composition he prefers. A melody harmonized several different ways might be useful for a learning situation or an attitude question; a short ABA form composition, with different B sections, could be used the same ways. Several different soprano voices on record singing the same song could be compared, instrumental qualities could be compared, and so forth.

2.0 Responding. A response is what the teacher works toward in teaching for affective growth, and until the student responds the teacher may feel that no objective in this area has been reached, because the previous levels are so tentative. Here the student becomes interested, thus laying the foundation for a real emotional response. The initial form of response is still relatively passive, characterized by acquiescence. From there the student develops a willingness to respond, and finally a true satisfaction in response, which will cause him to seek out musical experiences on his own.

2.1 Acquiescence in responding. At this level the student will play in the band or sing in the chorus at the suggestion of his parents or teacher. He will practice the same way as the result of a schedule or a suggestion. There may be little evidence of active pleasure in the doing, but there is absence of hostility or resistance. An attitude test for this level might be to list a number of musical acts such as practicing pieces, practicing scales and technical exercises, listening to music on the radio, listening to musical programs on television, joining in family music-making, participating in a church choir; the student is then asked to put the appropriate number by each act: (1) I do it without being told, (2) I do it when reminded, (3) I try to get out of doing it, (4) I don't do it even though people want me to, (5) I don't do it, and nobody objects. Other items could be added that indicate a greater involvement: listening to recordings of one's own instrument, listening to ensemble recordings in which one's instrument plays, checking out recordings from the public library (where appropriate), practicing band or ensemble or choir music at home.

2.2 Willingness to respond. Willingness indicates voluntary activity, a consent to the act, a greater cooperation than that implied by simple acquiescence. The orchestra or choir member will cooperate in being silent when the situation demands it, giving ideas or some other verbal response when these are solicited, and being responsible for his musical part during the rehearsal. The same sort of evaluative tool could be used for this category as for the preceding one, but the expected response at this level would be "I do it without being told," rather than "I do it when reminded." The line between acquiescence and willingness is fine; the category that follows, satisfaction, is where the real difference lies.

2.3 Satisfaction in response. The important new component here is the emotional response of pleasure, enjoyment, or delight. It would be misleading to suggest that the emotional response occurs just at this step, immediately following 2.2 and preceding 3.0. The recognition of satisfaction appears gradually through the levels already described, at some point becoming great enough to be a conscious factor in the student's reaction to music and musical situations. When emotional involvement takes place, the possibility is present for genuine aesthetic experiences in music, provided the necessary knowledge and understanding are also present. At this level, the student will actively seek out ways to promote satisfactory experiences in music. His tastes and preferences within music may not be firmly formed but he is aware that he "likes music" and therefore wants to participate in it. He will give up some other things to participate in musical performance or listening. A tool to help measure the arrival of this stage would list many activities in music, similar to those cited earlier but with greater specificity of choice, and ask the student to respond: "I like to do it very much"; "I like it somewhat"; "I do not care either way"; "I do not like to do it"; "I have never done it." The list could contain such differentiations as, for example, "going to a band concert," "going to a choir concert," "going to an orchestra concert," "going to a concert by a professional symphony orchestra." Answers would indicate what sort of discrimination was developing, beyond the simple fact of enjoyment. Music used in rehearsal could be the subject matter for a response list, the responses being: "Let's play it often until we learn it well"; "let's play it once in a while"; "I do not wish to play it again"; "I don't care either way."

3.0 Valuing. The act of valuing is the act of ascribing worth or merit to something. As the student comes to take pleasure in active response to music, he begins to acquire a belief in its value. He also begins to acquire a set of values that places more worth upon certain musical items than upon others. At first this set of values is adopted from that of the group or the community, and only later will it become individualized and made truly the person's own.

3.1 Acceptance of a value. Music teachers are concerned that values are taught. Objectives for music education commonly include emphasis upon students' valuing the musical heritage and understanding why composers are deemed great. The entire area of music appreciation focuses upon the valued works of the past and present and upon helping students to recognize that value. The first step in acquiring a value is to believe that it is real, although the actual experience of its value may not have taken place. The student accepts the teacher's statement that Beethoven is a great composer and that Beethoven symphonies are great works of art. He listens to these works in an attempt to hear some of what the teacher has been talking about. He retains much of the information given him about Beethoven and tries to apply it to the music he plays and hears. In this way he is giving himself the opportunity to experience the value; he accepts it as a belief and explores the objects that contain the value. As this process is followed for various areas of music, classical or others, the student deepens his familiarity and his understanding until he develops genuine preferences for certain values. The best way to measure the acceptance of a value is to examine the response made to it. Questions that ask for opinions and information about a piece of music or a composer can help to measure this area.

3.2 Preference for a value. As the student acts upon his acceptance of a value, he comes to the place where his preference for the value is real, no longer borrowed from authority or custom. He seeks it out, pursues it, advocates it to those who are uncommitted or skeptical. Perhaps he develops a real appreciation for contemporary music, among other kinds. He will ask his teacher for contemporary compositions to play, he will give up some other activity to attend a concert where contemporary music is performed. Perhaps he will argue the relative merits of modern music versus older forms in contention with his classmates or his teacher. He may have a number of values to which he gives preference over lesser likes; when these come into conflict with each other, then the manner in which he solves the conflict will strengthen some values for him and lessen others. Preference questions can help to measure this level. They will reveal more information if preference must be shown between several attractive alternatives than they will if one alternative is obviously more appealing than the others. Other tools, such as logs and critical incidence tests, are also appropriate.

3.3 Commitment. Commitment is here defined as conviction, or certainty beyond doubt. A loyalty to the value has developed, and the student attempts to convert others to his viewpoint. These are the attributes that initiate and encourage all kinds of movements. The committed student may try to persuade others who play an instrument to join the orchestra; he may organize a fund-raising drive for some musical purpose; he may on his own decide he should change to a private teacher known to be more demanding and particular than his present one; he may increase his practice time or purchase music and technique material not required by his teacher; he may organize a small ensemble in which he and others can perform. The student who looks forward to a professional career in music has made a commitment, and he may display some of the characteristics just mentioned. However, the same actions and the same commitment to music can be found in students whose career plans lie in other fields. The commitment to musical values at this level does not crowd out other commitments, but can exist side by side with them.

4.0 Organization. As the student grows in experience, he comes to hold a number of values, which he eventually must put into some sort of order or system. Situations will continually arise in which more than one value is relevant, and these values will compete and create conflict. To resolve the conflict, the individual will settle upon a hierarchy in which some values dominate and others become secondary. In order to develop a value system, some conceptualization of values must first take place.

4.1 Conceptualization of a value. Here the individual is able to think about a value, to examine it, abstract it and compare it with others he holds. He may not be able to do this verbally, but the affective aspect of the value is sufficiently clear that he knows its significance for himself. Actions which help identify this level might include: attempts to describe the characteristics of an art period which have meaning for him; attempts to state the qualities which make an admired symphony conductor great; descriptions of the aesthetic response as he has experienced it; judgments as to relative merits of composers or performers; attempts to recognize the changes within one composer's style.

4.2 Organization of a value system. The organization of a value system is typically associated with the college student, motivated toward several things at once, away from parental authority, which has previously influenced his decisions, finding conflicts rising from lack of time and energy to pursue all things at once and well. Ideally, the value system one adopts is harmonious and allows for ordered relationships. In fact, most persons continue to experience conflicts and shifts of value as new situations present themselves and new interests arise to compete with older ones. At this level we have come to the final portion of affective experience for which music teachers need to take some responsibility; they should continue to help students find the satisfactory place for music in their lives. Few students will feel it should have a central place in their hierarchy of values, but most students hopefully will feel a need for music as a value for their lives. To help measure this important level of development, one or more widely inclusive attitude scales such as the Hevner attitude scale, the MMPI (Minnesota Multiphasic Personality Inventory, a personality inventory that is comparable in quality to the Strong among interest measures), the Kuder Preference Record, or Strong's Vocational Interest Blank may be used.

5.0 *Characterization by a value or value complex.* This level represents the culmination of affective experiences into one strong and consistent philosophy of life. It can best be illustrated by the dedicated artist, scientist, statesman, teacher, or whatever, whose life and decisions all revolve around a single focus. The focus need not be professional, though it usually is; one may be dedicated to a value system and use his vocation only as a means to accomplish the values. Or one may have a value system that is essentially focused on human relations, so that any vocational and avocational activity that will fit into the value system will be acceptable to the individual. Music teaching does not include within its goals this level of development, though the music profession offers numerous examples of individuals whose values systems center around the musical experience. The two aspects of this level are, first (5.1) generalized set, and (5.2) the integration of these beliefs and values into a total philosophy or *world view*.

index